COLIN URQUHART: A BIOGRAPHY

COLIN URQUHART:
A BIOGRAPHY

John Peters

Hodder & Stoughton
LONDON SYDNEY AUCKLAND

This book is dedicated to my wife, Elisabeth, and our three children, Daniel, Kathy and Joanna, for all their love and support

First published in 1994 by Hodder and Stoughton Ltd.
a division of Hodder Headline PLC

10 9 8 7 6 5 4 3 2 1

British Library Cataloging in Publication Data

Peters, John
Colin Urquhart:Biography
I. Title
248.4092

ISBN 0 340 58040 2

Typeset by Hewer Text Composition Services, Edinburgh
Printed and bound in Great Britain by
Cox & Wyman Ltd, Reading, Berks.

Hodder and Stoughton Ltd
A division of Hodder Headline PLC
47 Bedford Square
London WC1B 3DP

CONTENTS

PROLOGUE

Colin Urquhart's birth was both normal *and* unusual. Normal because it was perfectly routine. Unusual because it was accompanied by a Roman Catholic nun's prophecy that he would be instrumental in comforting and encouraging God's people.

This encouragement has taken many forms since then: sermons, books, individual counsel and advice, kindness, and his personal example of integrity and determination. It also includes the tapes of his preaching, a fact powerfully demonstrated in the life of a young married woman we shall call Margaret.

Terminally ill with leukaemia, she was sent several of Colin's teaching tapes. They had an immediate and striking effect, as Margaret herself says:

> The words I heard built and re-affirmed my faith. Hearing those healing words in God's promises strengthened both myself and my husband, and brought us into a new awareness of God's wonderful mercy, His power to make all things possible, but most of all of the love of Jesus Christ who died on the cross *for me*.
>
> So many people, in their well-meaning way, told me of the way my illness had drawn them together, as they met and prayed for me. I began to believe that I was the sacrifice for their renewed fellowship.
>
> How wrong I was. Colin Urquhart's tapes showed me how Jesus had already made the one perfect sacrifice and how

presumptious it was of me to think I could do it too. It was by feeding on God's words that my eyes began to be opened and my spirit to soar like a bird, rather than being dragged down like a stone. *Hearing God's words for me through Colin Urquhart's tapes, I was transformed*!

The experience of this young woman, who was healed after the entry of God's Word through Colin, is but one illustration of how the nun's prophetic word has been fulfilled in his life.

INTRODUCTION

Colin Urquhart is a quiet, relaxed, shy, grey-haired Englishman in his early fifties. He is a father of three grown-up children, Claire, Clive and Andrea, all of whom are keen Christians, and a grandfather. He might well object to being called an 'Englishman' because he is 'by instinct a Scotsman'. Part of the explanation for this is the fact that his family hailed originally from Inverness. His instinctive sense of Scottishness, however, does not prevent him from being an avid supporter of the English cricket team: he got up at 4.30 a.m. to watch their unavailing efforts to win the World Cup in Australia in March 1992, and was disappointed by their defeat.

In private conversation Colin is gentle, unassertive, even diffident, seldom making statements, almost never referring to himself and his many activities. This diffidence belies the fact that he is one of the foremost Christian leaders in Britain today, with an influence stretching far beyond the confines of his base in Sussex and the coasts of Britain. This diffidence on a personal level is also markedly absent in his preaching, when he is firm, definite and authoritative. His authority is not the product of natural or innate ability; rather it is the result of the Holy Spirit working powerfully and dynamically in his life. It is also the result of listening to God's voice on a systematic, daily basis.

Colin is a man of many parts. There is, first, his rôle as Director of Kingdom Faith Ministries at Roffey Place in

Faygate, Horsham, West Sussex. The college has a number of experienced and well-known people on the staff, including Michael Barling (formerly Director of the Fountain Trust), but Colin is overwhelmingly accepted as 'the Boss', not that he would ever use this description himself. Lots of students come to the college precisely because Colin is there. They are eager to learn from him principles of faith, holiness and healing, three fundamental emphases of his ministry. From this base his itinerant ministry takes him throughout the world: to date, he has preached in thirty countries. Nowadays his travelling is largely confined to the college vacations, but on such travels he is sometimes accompanied by teams of students who are keen to witness, at first hand, how faith operates within the context of an international preaching ministry.

He is also a best-selling author; by the end of 1992 he had written twelve books.[1] It is a prodigious output for someone who has to fit his writing in between the many other calls on his time and energies. Colin's books often grow out of his preaching. For example, *In Christ Jesus* and *Holy Fire* were preached to the community at the Hyde long before they appeared in print. Some of his books have sold in huge numbers, including *When the Spirit Comes*, *My Father is the Gardener* and *Receive Your Healing*, but they have all been outstripped by *My Dear Child* which was reprinted five times within the first six months of publication. Later we shall look at and analyse the reasons for this success.

Colin's advice and counsel are constantly sought on a range of Christian issues, frequently by people who once worked with him and have moved on elsewhere, while an Urquhart 'foreword' is often enough to give a new book a flying start.

He is also considered to be a leading figure in the healing ministry, a New Testament emphasis that features prominently amongst charismatic Christians. He seldom refers to his meetings as 'healing meetings' *per se*, but he always expects God to demonstrate and vindicate His Word in signs and wonders. As he says in *The Positive Kingdom*,

> Those first disciples saw the power of God at work as they went out to proclaim the gospel of the Kingdom. They did not go out as healers, miracle-workers or as those seeking signs as ends in themselves. They went out with the Kingdom message, but expected their words to be confirmed by God with demonstration of Kingdom power. They expected to see signs following the preaching of the Word.[2]

Colin's attitude to healing mirrors exactly the precedents set by our Lord's disciples.

The initial evidence suggests that Colin Urquhart wields considerable influence. He is widely respected, and his preaching and writing ministry has affected the lives of thousands of people both at home and abroad. Nor does he show any sign of letting up; indeed his enthusiasm for God's work is as great as ever it was. To begin to appreciate how all this came about, we need to consider some of the main developments in his life, beginning at Twickenham in the early years of the Second World War.

1

EARLY DAYS

Colin Urquhart was born on January 26th, 1940 at the family home in Twickenham, Middlesex, the eldest son of Kenneth and Lillian Urquhart. His entire childhood was spent in the same house in this essentially middle-class area. He has one brother, Barry, now an architect and living in Walton-on-Thames, and one sister, Pauleen, a nurse married to a doctor and living on the Isle of Wight.

Kenneth, an architect, came from a Scottish family, as the name Urquhart implies. His family had moved south to England from Inverness in the early part of the twentieth century, a move dictated by Colin's grandfather's search for employment. So Kenneth, though conceived in Scotland, was born and brought up in Wimbledon. On his father's side of the family, Colin comes from a long line of architects and artists.

Lillian's father was a sailor and had joined the Royal Navy at the age of twelve when ships were still steam and sail. He often talked about 'climbing the rigging'. He was a dynamic and colourful character who used to sit Colin on his knee and regale him with stories about his sailing days. He lived to the grand old age of ninety-seven and until two years before his death would think nothing of walking several miles each day.

Colin's background was thus an amalgam of Scottish ruggedness and durability, on the one hand, with inventiveness, imagination and artistic ability, on the other. It is not difficult to see why Colin is so determined, yet so keen on painting and music. His forebears' genes are happily at work in him.

Education

His early education was received at a small preparatory school in Twickenham called The Mall which, like preparatory schools to this day, prepared its pupils for public school. In Colin's case it was for St Paul's School, then in West Kensington and now in Barnes. His brother and sister were also educated privately, an outlay made possible only through considerable sacrifice on the part of Kenneth and Lillian. They both believed this was the best education available and were thus happy to make those sacrifices.

Colin went to St Paul's in 1953, Coronation Year, staying there for three years, and obtaining five passes at the then G.C.E. Ordinary Level. He left the school two terms later; the financial pressure on his father was enormous and Colin knew that to leave St Paul's would help to relieve the financial burden for the whole family. The school offered the Urquharts a bursary because they wanted Colin to stay, but he realised that his parents would not feel comfortable with this proposal. A further reason for his somewhat premature departure was that Colin's father wanted him to pursue a career in architecture. Although Colin knew deep in his heart that one day he would be ordained, he was at that time prepared to go along with his father's wishes. So he spent the summer months of 1957 studying at home and doing a great deal of draughtsmanship, since his father believed that the most profitable way to prepare for an architectural career was to gain practical experience by working in a firm, pursuing whatever was necessary by way of academic study at night school. Kenneth was quite opposed to academic architects who gained their degrees at university but whose grasp of the practical realities of the profession (for example, the cost of putting designs into effect), was less assured. So Colin went to work for a firm who were architects to a brewery. He comments laconically: 'I spent eighteen months of my life going round many pubs in the East End of London especially and learning the trade the hard way.' He was not destined to be an architect, however.

Christian influences

Colin's Christian experience began at approximately the age of nine when he began to wonder, 'Why has God made me?' There was no Christian background in his family as far as he is aware. Certainly his parents were not Christians, although they both made a commitment to the Lord Jesus in their seventies. So at that time his father was unable to answer Colin's philosophical and theological musings, and so began a determined quest for spiritual certainty. This quest included praying from a book of prayers but also listening to God for direction and guidance. This process culminated in God 'breaking through with a sense of glory' (Colin's words). At that time he knew nothing whatsoever of the Gospel in any formal or theological sense, though he did appreciate that he had, as he puts it himself, 'met with the Lord' in a highly significant, life-changing way. What is interesting about this experience is that it is not expressed in the usual evangelical terminology of repentance, forgiveness and conversion. Colin had quite simply experienced God in a comprehensive and transforming way, so much so that it defied all formulas, all neat explanations, all attempts to reduce it to a rigid pattern. He was only nine at this time, but what occurred was utterly different from comprehending God in Sunday School terms, as is frequently the case with nine-year-olds. God had broken into his life in a direct, personal way, changing it for ever.

The idea of becoming an Anglican priest was first formed

four years later, when Colin was thirteen. He was a member of the choir at his local parish church and one day the Vicar told him that the Bishop had started what was called a 'fellowship of vocation' for those who were interested in being ordained some time in the future. Although the minimum age was sixteen, the Vicar had written a letter to the Bishop asking if Colin could be allowed to join this newly-formed fellowship as it was obvious that he would be ordained. What was obvious to the Vicar was not at that stage obvious to Colin. He did, though, go away and think about the Vicar's initiative and concluded that he (the Vicar) was right. So he went along to the 'fellowship of vocation' meetings, each person being assigned a tutor with whom he met regularly. These occasions had no discernible influence on his life and thinking in general, but they kept alive within him the idea of ordination until the time of his architectural apprenticeship.

Divine impulsion

By the age of seventeen Colin knew with certainty what God was saying. 'I just knew that I had to leave architecture and take the necessary steps. The only reason for this was that God was calling me. I didn't have any great or exalted notion of how God would use me or anything like that. I certainly didn't have any desire to be a priest or to be ordained.' This definite sense of God's call on his life has remained with Colin throughout his ministry. It gives comfort and reassurance. It also motivates and equips him, and imparts resolve and determination. Once he was sure that God was calling him he took the necessary steps to leave the firm he was working for.

He also applied for what was then known as CACTM (Church's Advisory Committee on Training and Ministry), which led to a selection conference for aspiring ordinands, held at Farnham Castle, one of the old palaces of the Bishop of

Winchester. He was duly accepted for training, the only proviso being that he first went to university. Colin was reluctant to pursue this course of action, not least because he had never had any desire for a university education. As it was a condition of acceptance, however, he had little choice. He studied by correspondence for A Levels in Religious Knowledge and English Literature, and enrolled as a student at King's College in the University of London in 1959.

The only other fleeting ambition he had at this time was to play cricket professionally, but as he knew that he would never have made the grade at this level of the game, cricket remained something he enjoyed as a hobby, and still does today.

King's College, London

Colin spent four years at King's College reading Theology. It was not an easy time for him. He had a strong relationship with God in prayer, but had no biblical understanding, either to provide a conceptual framework for his faith, or to combat the liberal theology that was his staple diet as an undergraduate. In fact, King's Faculty of Theology was probably the most liberal in the whole country at the time. The inevitable result was that he absorbed quite a lot of the teaching. 'Being a frightened sort of person I didn't question things too much. I sat, listened and absorbed what was told me.'

For the first two years at King's Colin lived at home, travelling up to London daily as his lecture programme dictated. For his third year he was required to live in the College's residential hostel at Westminster. During this academic year he sat for, and passed, his Associateship of King's College (AKC), after which came a year's pastoral training at St Boniface, Warminster, at that time a theological college attached to King's College. The course trained students to preach, administer the sacraments and counsel people. Such training was largely based on modern

9

psychological techniques, but Colin views that year (1962–63) positively: 'It meant that during my last year there weren't any exams and I could devote myself to a consideration of practical pastoral issues. It was also a time when I could spend quite a bit of time in prayer.'

His calling confirmed

February 1963 at St Boniface was a crucial month for him. He was convinced that what God was asking of him in being ordained was a huge mistake, as he considered himself to be 'the wrong kind of person altogether'. He shut himself away in the College chapel one afternoon and told God that if He really wanted him to go through with the business of ordination, He 'would have to do something'. Do something He certainly did, as Colin records in *When the Spirit Comes*: 'I started to breathe very heavily for a few minutes, and then suddenly was filled with a great peace. God was breathing his Holy Spirit into me. I found myself speaking strange words, a language that I did not know. It never occurred to me that I was "speaking in tongues". I did not understand it.'[1]

Colin only had a limited appreciation of what was happening to him, even less of its significance. In addition, he had never heard of the charismatic movement, which had hardly begun in 1963. He was naturally perplexed and so consulted a member of the staff at the college, who didn't understand Colin's experience either and offered a psychological explanation of what had occurred. This was not at all helpful, but Colin knew in his own mind, from that moment in the chapel, that he could proceed with ordination.

As with his conversion, he did not receive the baptism of the Spirit with any preconceived or predetermined ideas. It simply happened to him, and from day one he accepted it as a natural part of the Christian life. This infusion of the Holy Spirit has to be accompanied by Submission to Him, a theme which Colin was later to emphasise in his preaching and writing: 'This is God's order for your life: your soul submitted to His Spirit, so that rivers of living water flow out of your life.'[2]

Despite his confidence to go forward with the process of ordination, there still remained the question of how he would deal with the daily life of a parish, and how he would put into practice the principles of faith in a consistent and practical way. His first parish, in Cheshunt, proved to be a great challenge.

2

THE YOUNG CURATE

It is an axiom that curates are meant to make their worst mistakes in their first parish. Certainly, to deal with the problems of the real world after the rarefied atmosphere of university and theological college comes as a shock to many young priests, and Colin was no exception, though he had gained some practical pastoral experience at Warminster. As curate at Cheshunt, he was expected to look after the sick and housebound in the parish, in addition to the many other routine duties of parish life. He found people sympathetic and pleased to see him, though he soon found that his liberal theology was of little practical help in difficult situations. He felt utterly inadequate. Yet, insistently, a small but definite voice within him kept urging him to 'heal the sick'. Because he didn't know how to heal the sick, he consulted his Vicar, whose response was one of bemused embarrassment. He obviously had no more idea of how to deal with his parishioners than did Colin.

The beginning of a healing ministry

Colin decided to form a group specifically to ask God how to heal the sick. God spoke to him directly: 'I will teach you myself when you believe it; whatever you believe, you will *see* happening.' From this point onwards the Holy Spirit became his teacher, and he saw the need to believe all the Bible, not just those parts predetermined by denominational bias. Gradually, and helped by the books of Watchman Nee (the Chinese preacher for so long incarcerated in Chinese jails for his faith), Colin related understanding the Word of God to its outworking in daily life and experience: theology encouraging faith. As he prayed and studied, he began to see healing in a much wider context than simply physical healing. As he writes in *Receive Your Healing*, 'God wants you to be spiritually healthy as well as emotionally and physically healthy. His purpose for you is "wholeness". Your emotional and physical health depend to a very large extent on your spiritual well-being.'[1]

Very soon after these revelations, Colin had an opportunity to put his faith into practice. He was brought into contact with a young woman suffering from inoperable cancer of the bowel. Her prospects were clearly bleak. How would Colin respond to this real-life dilemma? Pray for her 'soul', ask God if it was his will to heal her? He said none of these safe things; instead he found himself saying, with authority and confidence, 'Jesus will heal you.' The amazing fact is that such a phrase had never crossed his lips before. After prayer, however, and the laying on of hands, she was completely healed, and is alive today.

At this stage, too, Colin's, life began to change radically in altogether more personal ways.

A blind date

October 8th, 1963, was an important milestone in Colin's life. Invited out to supper by one of his parishioners, he met Caroline May, who was born in 1940 in the village of Meldreth, ten miles south of Cambridge. Her family background had not been entirely happy or even settled. At the age of three her mother went into hospital and never returned to her husband and children (Diana, David and Caroline). Subsequently her parents separated and she only saw her mother on two further occasions. This separation had another consequence, too: Caroline's father was cold-shouldered at the local Anglican church.

Caroline's early life was uneventful. She attended Sunday School at the local Anglican church but derived nothing from it in terms of a personal, living relationship with God. Nor she have any clear idea of the distinctive emphases of Christianity. She was christened and later confirmed at the age of thirteen largely because of the pressure exerted by her family and church, and because it was an open door to take communion. God seemed remote from her – a vague being elsewhere – and as she grew older she attended church only on festivals like Christmas and Easter.

Caroline didn't get much enjoyment from her school life either. Educated at the local village school until the age of eleven, she proceeded, via success in the Eleven Plus Examination, to the (then) Cambridge High School for Girls. It was a school with a high academic reputation, but having contrived to fail all her O Level examinations, except cookery, she left school in 1957 to work in a large store in Cambridge selling women's clothes. Later, at the age of twenty-one, she trained as a manageress with a firm selling women's and children's clothes in Harlow, Essex. She acquired a car and, on the evening of October 8th, 1963, drove over to her cousin's home in Cheshunt where the recently arrived curate (one Colin Urquhart) was also a guest for supper.

The evening was a great success: 'Colin was skinny all right, and had come straight from work in his clergy gear with a grey floppy jumper over the top, so he fitted the image. What I hadn't expected, stupidly now I realise, was that he was human, with a great sense of humour. We had a relaxed, hilarious evening.'[2] Mutual attraction soon led to their first formal date, an outing to the show, 'Beyond the Fringe' and a meal. By June 1964 (the month Colin was ordained a priest) they were engaged, with the wedding fixed for October 24th, 1964.

Since by this time Caroline had not been to church for years, she was relieved that nothing was expected of her by the parish, though of course she attended the main weekly services. Being a curate's wife was, for the most part, an undemanding rôle, in contrast to the many and varied demands placed upon Colin, who was extremely busy.

Soon, however, Caroline was fully occupied with domestic concerns, as their first child, Claire, was born in 1965, to be followed by Clive in 1967 and Andrea in 1970.

Colin remained at Cheshunt for three-and-a-half years altogether, after which he moved to become Priest-in-charge at St Thomas's Church, Letchworth, near Hitchin, Hertfordshire.

During his years at Cheshunt Colin had conducted marriages, taken funerals, led confirmation classes, preached, given communion and generally acquainted himself with the full range of duties and activities expected of an Anglican priest. He had learned to minister to the sick, lonely and depressed and those undergoing difficulties and tensions in their Christian lives. With the move to Letchworth, his ministry changed in two particular ways.

Changes in his preaching

With three sermons to deliver each Sunday, Colin's preaching load was heavy, and required a great deal of reading and preparation. One Sunday Colin preached from prepared notes in the morning service but had simply been too tired to prepare for Evensong. The previous evening he had shut himself away in the church and felt God saying 'Trust me.' Trusting though he tried to be, throughout the formal liturgical parts of Evensong he was, quite literally, 'in a cold sweat': he was terrified of what was – or was not – going to happen next. The hymn before the sermon came and went, he then prayed, more in anguish than faith, and stood up to preach.

What followed astounded him. Words flowed effortlessly from his mouth, accompanied by the distinct impression that he was standing beside himself listening to his own words, which continued to cascade forth. He found the experience exhilarating, and the congregation seemed responsive to this new approach. He decided to repeat it the following Sunday evening, hoping that it would be equally thrilling: and it was. The effect on the church was remarkable: within a very short time the congregation had doubled on Sunday evenings. Colin confessed his bemusement: 'I can't understand it; the evening services are so very different.' The Church Warden, however, said: 'It's because the sermons are so different.' Three aspects of his preaching at these evening services are worth noting. First, the sermons were not controlled by preparation beforehand. This is not to suggest that sermons should not be prepared properly and fully, rather that an element outside the control – and possible restriction – of the mind had come into operation: the direct influence of the Holy Spirit through a channel (Colin) who, in human terms, had no more to give. Second, the sermon caused the congregation to think seriously about the relationship between faith and daily behaviour: the sermons required a response of the hearers. Lastly, the preaching created an aura of excitement which had not been apparent in the more formally conducted morning services.

Colin pondered these occasions carefully, and began to perceive something of the true nature of preaching, which he defines in the following way: 'It has to be accompanied by a response in the hearts of the people. It has to be followed by Holy Spirit events in the lives of those who respond: He makes things happen.'

It was not only in his preaching that Colin was developing at this time; he was also growing in his understanding.

Changes in his understanding

Though outwardly successful, and able in particular to win the trust and confidence of young people, Colin considered that he had failed them because of his inability to bring them to the point of conversion, of being born again. He lacked the confidence to lead them from being aware of the Gospel to a definite response of faith.

It was at this period that he read *The Normal Christian Life*, one of Watchman Nee's most influential books. This book is a consideration of certain key passages from the Epistle to the Romans, with special attention paid to the cross and resurrection of the Lord Jesus. Thus in chapter seven Nee deals with what he calls 'The Eternal Purpose', the great goal and objective of the whole of creation. Two extracts are particularly pertinent. The first is a comment on Romans 3:23:

> We read: 'All have sinned, and fall short of the glory of God.' God's purpose for man was glory, but sin thwarted that purpose by causing man to miss God's glory. When we think of sin we instinctively think of the judgement it brings; we invariably associate it with condemnation and hell. Man's thought is always of the punishment that will come to him if he sins, but God's thought is always of the glory man will miss if he sins. The result of sin is that we forfeit God's glory: the result of redemption is that we are qualified again for glory. God's purpose in redemption is glory, glory, glory.[3]

The second deals with John 1:14:

> We are told that the Lord Jesus was God's only begotten Son: 'The Word became flesh, and dwelt among us (and we beheld his glory, glory as of the only begotten from the Father).' That He was God's only begotten Son signifies that God had no other Son but this one. He was with the Father from all eternity. But, we are told, God was not satisfied that Christ should remain the only begotten Son; He wanted also to make Him His first begotten.

How could an only begotten Son become a first begotten? The answer is simple: by the Father having more children. If you have but one son, then he is the only begotten, but if thereafter you have other children, then the only begotten becomes the first begotten.

The divine purpose in creation and redemption was that God should have many children. He wanted *us*, and could not be satisfied without us.[4]

The result of reading Nee's book was that, under the guidance of the Holy Spirit, Colin realised that he had entered into a totally new relationship with God:

> This book made me realise that nearly everything I had known and experienced about the Christian life was 'sub-normal' . . . God was often portrayed to be great but remote; to be believed in, to be worshipped, but definitely not to be experienced in a personal way . . . Now something was happening to me . . . I was bubbling over with joy. It seemed as if the whole room, the whole house, everyone and everything around me had changed. I wanted to go on dancing and skipping around the house shouting 'I'm a son of God! I'm a son of God! I AM A SON OF GOD!'[5]

Colin's discovery of this fundamental New Testament truth transformed his whole life and ministry. He now found that he could minister, preach, love and heal precisely because he had the authority of a son of God. The Word of God had to pierce his thinking before it affected his emotions in an outward and exuberant way. His desire to skip, sing and dance must not be construed as over-emotional behaviour, or some kind of extravagant loss of control. Rather, he was submitting his emotion to the Spirit's influence. In *Personal Victory* he develops this thought in the following way:

> The one who depends on feelings rather than the Lord, only believes the presence of God if he 'feels' His presence. He believes His love, only if he 'feels' that love. He obeys the

19

Word, if he 'feels' it right to do so. When his feelings are negative because of problems, he quickly panics or even falls into despair. He can easily be made to feel condemned by the enemy's false accusations.

It is impossible to live by faith when so dependent on feelings. Often the emotional response to a situation will be the opposite to a faith response. The Christian is called to believe the Lord, not his feelings. Every day of my life I have to walk in victory over emotional feelings. So do you!

When the soul is submitted to the Spirit, the feelings are influenced by the Lord but do not control the believer's decisions. The over-emotional frequently place the soul above the Spirit.

The emotionally insecure are usually spiritually insecure, because they pay so much attention to feelings. Those who are prone to feel rejected may well have problems believing the Lord has accepted them. Those who have felt the need to be self-dependent because they have found it difficult to trust others will find it difficult to trust the Lord. Those who have tried to manipulate others will try to manipulate the Lord.

The Lord does not want your emotions to govern you; He wants you to govern your emotions.

This is possible, even if you have been over-emotional, either through fear or an over-dependence on experience.[6]

Colin's realisation that he was a son of God gave him a security and a dignity that remain with him to this day. It also increased his love for God; prayer became a delight rather than a grudging and burdensome chore, and he felt God speaking to him personally as he read the Bible. He felt free in a totally new way, towards God, towards Jesus, his family and other people. Shortly after this increase in his spiritual and theological understanding Colin moved to St Hugh's, Luton. He could not have anticipated – and nor could Caroline – the momentous events that lay ahead, a voyage of discovery in every sense of that phrase.

3

ST HUGH'S, LEWSEY

The Suffragan Bishop of Hertford considered the parish of St Hugh's, Lewsey to be a challenging job. Given that high-ranking churchmen often resort to understatement, the word 'challenging' may be reinterpreted 'very demanding and difficult'. There were several reasons for this, not least the fact that the church was situated on the edge of Luton's industrial complex which is dominated by the massive Vauxhall motor works. There was a generally tepid response to what went on in the church, while a number of its more dedicated members were severely disillusioned. 'Is there more to church life than merely raising money for buildings?' Colin was asked, an obvious reference to the new church building, built after years of fund raising. He longed to reply to this pertinent question by saying that church members were meant to be living in the daily power of the Holy Spirit.

So tough and rigorous was the parish that two of Colin's immediate predecessors had been troubled by ill health. Indeed when asked to move to Luton, Colin was assured that five years was the longest he could anticipate being in the parish. Not surprisingly, he questioned the wisdom of leaving St Thomas's, Letchworth, where his preaching had undergone such a transformation, where the church had earned the reputation of being alive and innovative, and where the work amongst the young people was both successful and productive. On a personal level, too, Colin and Caroline now had three children, the youngest of them, Andrea, only just born. With such a young family, he scarcely needed a parish with a host of difficulties, but that's what he inherited in April 1970. The prospects were not promising, but just before the Urquhart family moved to Luton a significant event occurred.

The youngest child in the family, Andrea, had been born with imperfectly formed hips and so her bones clicked. A frame in the form of a cross was used to keep her legs apart and to prevent her hips from moving freely. The doctors hoped this device would cure the problem within a short period of time, but when Caroline took Andrea to the consultant three weeks after her birth, he shook his head sadly:

> 'I want you to understand that this doesn't always work,' he said. 'I'm afraid there are no signs of improvement.'

> 'What does that mean?' Caroline asked.

> 'It means that her movement will be impaired until she is eighteen months old. She will then have surgery and will be in plaster for some time. After that she will need calipers, and will have to learn to walk.'

> Caroline was in tears when she came back from the hospital. There was only one thing for it – prayer.[1]

The following week the same doctor examined Andrea thoroughly:

> 'Well,' he said with a smile, 'she seems to be fine. I'll put you in touch with the consultant at Luton who can keep an eye on her. As far as I am concerned she doesn't need that frame any more.'

> The other consultant confirmed that Andy's hip joints seemed sound enough. He suggested that we continued to use the frame for another few weeks 'just to be on the safe side'. We didn't mind that; we knew the Lord had healed her.[2]

The prayers had worked. Andrea had been healed. This event

encouraged Colin and Caroline and prepared them for the work ahead.

Colin's ministry at St Hugh's may be divided into three phases: the initial ferment of renewal (1970–71), growth and change (1972–74), and widening circles of influence (1974–75).[3]

Initial ferment

The early days at St Hugh's were ones of challenge and upheaval:

> I felt that we were all about to set out on a great adventure together. None of us knew where we were going or what the journey would be like. Deep within was the conviction that it was going to be different from anything I had known. God Himself was very definitely going to be in charge. I soon discovered that experiencing the power of the Holy Spirit in my life meant that I was also aware of God leading me in a much more positive and direct way than I had known before.

> My first sermon was about Jesus walking on the water. When Peter called to Jesus from the boat: 'Lord, if it is you, bid me come to you on the water', Jesus simply replied: 'Come'. The decision was Peter's. He could stay in the safety and security of the boat, or he could get out, keep his eyes fixed on Jesus and walk. 'I am going to get out of the boat,' I said, 'and I hope that some of you will come with me.'[4]

Many people did come with him, but first they had to learn that a Christian 'is someone who allows God to do something for him', and this includes facing the truth that a living relationship with Jesus Christ is only possible with the dynamic experience of the Holy Spirit at a *personal* level.

The first meeting of the Church Council, held in the lounge of Colin and Caroline's house, was certainly different from the norm. Instead of concentrating on matters of business, organisation, finances and future planning, it revolved around the question 'What is a Christian?' Many of the members of the Church Council were successful in their careers, and inevitably some of them were resistant to such a line of enquiry, and Colin searched desperately for an illustration to explain how God deals with a person's 'old life' and comes into lives in the power of the Holy Spirit. Rather dramatically he left the room and headed swiftly for the adjoining kitchen:

'A teapot. Quick! I must have a teapot!' I said to Caroline, who had just finished putting the children to bed.

'It's full of tea leaves,' she said.

'Haven't we another one?'

'What do you want it for?'

'I can't explain now. What about this old coffee-pot? I can use that.'

I rushed back to the lounge with it. 'Every human being is like a coffee-pot,' I began. 'Imagine that there's a certain amount of liquid in this pot, representing the natural human power and resources that each of us has; our ability to work, to think, to love, to talk, to bring up our children and so on.

'Because we have free-will, we can tilt our coffee-pot in any direction whenever we please, and out of the spout will flow some of the liquid. In other words, we will use some of the resources within us to do whatever we have to do. That is a human being; but not a Christian. The trouble with this character is that he can use the resources already within him, but his lid is firmly on. Nothing more can be poured into him.

'If you have ever tried to fill a pot with the lid on, you will know that the water flows over the outside of the pot, and all you get is a mess.'

I went on: 'Most people's spiritual lives are like that – a mess. And that can even be said of many church-goers. They try

24

to serve God in their own strength, instead of allowing Him
to remove the lid and pour His life and strength into them.
This is what God wants to do for each one of us: to pour
His love into us, not over us. He wants to give to us all the
blessings that only He can give.

'It is obviously important that this lid is removed, because
it is acting like a barrier keeping God out of our lives.
No wonder the Christian life seems like a hard struggle to
us, if we are trying to know Him and serve Him with our
lids on!'

Everybody was following this illustration intently. I continued: 'St Paul calls this lid the "self" – that naturally
sinful, selfish, self-centred part of us that says: "My life
is my own to do what I like with. I know what I want
and I am going to have what I want. I am going to be
lord and master of my own life." I . . . me . . . my . . .
self . . .

'God wants to remove that lid, that old self, so that He can
come flowing into our lives.'[5]

Predictably some of his hearers were astounded, perplexed,
even angry, but a seed of truth and faith had been sown in
their hearts. They warmed to the idea of a new and vibrant
relationship with God, something possible only through the
Holy Spirit; and they understood that the invigorating power
of the Holy Spirit was necessary for their lives each day. Colin
also pointed out that God wanted St Hugh's to be part of
His continuing ministry to the world, 'part of his earthly,
spirit-filled Body.'

For a number of the parishioners, this teaching meant
a radical shift in their spiritual and biblical understanding.
In some cases, the effect of the shift was tantamount to
that of an earthquake, thoroughly altering their perspectives,
sweeping away old ideas and comfortable truths to which they
had long held.

Colin realised that if he was to bring about what amounted

to a revolution, he had first to lay a firm foundation of biblical teaching and explanation. Like Martyn Lloyd-Jones, he knew that theology and doctrine must be given precedence, and this he tried to do in the early days at St Hugh's. Renewal, still less revival, was not possible until people had an understanding of the character and working of God. Illustrations such as the one about the coffee-pot were not simply chosen at random, but were used to bring home biblical truths. They had the crucial advantage of being both ordinary and also visually graphic. Like a good teacher, Colin knew the value of an illustration in imprinting truths in people's minds. So at the outset of his ministry at St Hugh's he sought to make people think about their faith in different and innovative ways.

But the teaching in itself was unlikely to trigger renewal in the life of the church. A movement of the Holy Spirit was needed too, and early one evening a tall, bearded Welshman called Gomer barged his way unceremoniously into Colin's study.

'It's no use,' he began, 'I can't wait – I must be filled with the Holy Spirit. How can I get rid of my lid – tonight!'

Gomer could be a very determined man!

Well, this is it; the crunch for me! 'You talked about it, Colin,' I thought, 'now you have to do it: lead this man to a relationship with Jesus, and to a full experience of the Holy Spirit. Lord, please help me.'

'Gomer, all that belongs to that lid has to be given to Jesus.'

'Right,' said Gomer. 'How?'

'I have to go out for about half an hour, Gomer. Go into church, sit quietly and ask the Lord to show you everything that you need to offer Him. Write it all down, the sins, fears and doubts of the past and and sort of person you are now. Open every area of your life to God, the good as well as the bad. He will take the rubbish and deal with it; He also needs to have your time and abilities at His disposal. When I come back from my appointment I will come and pray with you about all this.'

'Do you mean to say you want me to write down all that lot! And then let you pray with me about it? Never!' Gomer could also be stubborn.

'If you want Jesus to fill you with His Spirit, Gomer, He needs to have all of you.'

He hesitated. 'Well, it had better be worth it.'

'It will be,' I promised.

My appointment involved me more deeply than I had anticipated, and it was about ten fifteen before I returned to the church. I hardly expected to find Gomer still there. He was – kneeling at the altar rail.

'Colin, I am such a sinner,' he said as I approached.

In the following minutes, Gomer poured his heart out to God, amid his tears. I prayed that the Lord would forgive him, take away his fears, and heal him in body, mind and spirit. I laid hands on his head and prayed that the Lord Jesus would fill him to overflowing with His Holy Spirit.

There was a great sense of peace as we quietly thanked the Lord together.

'I will leave you to be alone with the Lord,' I said.

Gomer didn't stay long. He couldn't keep still! He rushed home to Audrey, his wife, and Adrian, their younger son, bubbling over with joy. He told them what had happened and how wonderful Jesus was.[6]

Gomer had become a witness not only to the love of the Lord Jesus but also to the new life that is the particular product of the Holy Spirit. As Colin put it, 'the renewal of our church had begun.'

Growth and change

Following from Gomer's experience, the 'Know Jesus' groups which had been established earlier by Colin began to proliferate. Some broken relationships began to be repaired, while the release of God's power was also demonstrated in a number of physical healings. Of the many examples that could be cited, two must suffice to illustrate what was a new phenomenon at St Hugh's church.

Stella was a school teacher, an active member of the Church Council, and a keen participant in the very first 'Know Jesus' group formed in the parish. For fourteen years, ever since the birth of her daughter Gillian, she had suffered from an incurable kidney complaint. It was both distressing and uncomfortable, but she was told by her doctors that she would have to live with the pain and make the best of her situation. Gradually, though, she came to believe that God could and would heal her and agreed to meet Colin for prayer one day after school. This is what happened next:

> We prayed together, praising God for all His love and goodness. I laid hands on Stella and prayed that He would heal her. She looked radiant and just began thanking the Lord. Apart from the kidney disease, Stella was suffering from arthritis in the neck and rheumatic pains in different parts of her body. As she praised, the discomfort began to disappear.[7]

Stella was completely healed of the aches and pains of the kidney disease as well. Her healing, not unnaturally, gave encouragement to the developing ministry of healing. The approach adopted, when compared with the often rumbustious tactics employed by some charismatics today, seems restrained and conservative:

> Unless there was great urgency, we always had a few days'

28

preparation before we prayed for healing. During this time we would take hold of the healing promises from the Bible, and ask the Lord to show us anything about ourselves that He wanted to change and to heal. We are told in the Gospel that Jesus healed all who came to Him. So we recognised the need for us to come to Him, to bring our whole selves to be healed, not just our physical ailments.[8]

Healing was thus viewed as an integral part of God's desire to impart wholeness to people's lives – physical, emotional, psychological and, of course, spiritual; and all against a background of mutual love, mutual acceptance and mutual caring for each other. Reading the account of these early days in *When the Spirit Comes*, I am struck by the absence of triumphalism and hype. Colin consistently taught the church that *Jesus* was the healer, rather than any particular method of persuasion or manipulation. It seemed a natural accompaniment to the truth of God's Word and the power of the gospel.

Pauline's case was more complex than Stella's. A young housewife, married and with four children, she was the only member of her family to attend church. Church did not seem to be very beneficial to her, however, because her life was decimated by feelings of guilt and fear. She considered herself to be 'unclean' and was forever washing her hands in an attempt to assuage those debilitating feelings, but to no avail. Her besetting fear was that other people would notice that she was unclean, especially the members of her own family. Two things happened to her. First she was filled with the Holy Spirit, and then she was healed of the inner doubts and fears which had so ruined her life and had obviously made her extremely difficult to live with. The difference in her life was marked at every level, and she wrote to Colin to express her thanks:

That other person who was me, no longer exists – is dead, finished, forgotten! IT IS NOT I WHO LIVE BUT CHRIST WHO LIVES WITHIN ME . . .

He accepted me, He welcomed me, He stretched out His
arms and took that old sinful person that was me upon the
cross that I might die with Him. He gave me new life, His
life, His joy, His happiness, His peace.

My heart sings. Jesus takes it all away – all the pain, all the
guilt, all the mistakes . . .

Already wonderful things have started to happen to me, my
life is richer, happier. I seem to be surrounded by love! All
the love that He is pouring into my life is overflowing into
other people's lives and they are responding to it, warming
to it, answering it.[9]

After the healing of her neurosis, Pauline found her relationships beginning to improve, not least with her children
and husband. Within a few months all three of her children
were converted and filled with the Holy Spirit. 'Pauline's
experience', says Colin, 'is a good example of the power of
God's forgiveness, the greatest act of healing in the lives of
His people.'

These healings coincided with a marked increase in the size
of the congregation at St Hugh's, and an air of excitement
pervaded the church's life. There was a great thirst for the
Word of God. The gifts of the Spirit (including speaking in
tongues) operated throughout the church, not least among the
children. Conversions were a regular occurrence, and prayer
and praise were abundantly in evidence. It would not be an
exaggeration to say that a spirit of renewal was infusing the
whole church with life, confidence and vision. Disillusionment
was a thing of the past: St Hugh's had come alive in the Spirit
in a way that affected the corporate life of the church, not just
individual lives.

Changes became apparent in the church's worship. The
main Sunday service was the nine-thirty Parish Communion.
A heightened sense of praise and worship started to emerge
at this service, although its form remained largely unchanged
and traditional. Neither Colin nor the congregation wanted to

alter its form because he was convinced that God wanted the church to remain united, and that unity should be expressed in the Parish Communion: change was not to be initiated for change's sake.

Attendance at Evensong was very small: It seemed to have little appeal, but then the Church Council agreed to a new form of service called 'Evening Praise'. The thinking behind this development was that people would be freer to express themselves in praise: 'the entire service was unstructured, so that we could allow the Holy Spirit to lead us', says Colin. Lasting for approximately an hour and a half, 'Evening Praise' was notable for its variety and flexibility. It included plenty of opportunity for meditating on the Word of God, the sermons were brief, children of all ages were welcome, and the whole service was joyful. Within a month the congregation in the evening had doubled to about eighty people, rising to a hundred and fifty within six months.

Colin was working incredibly hard; at the same time he felt fulfilled. This sense of fulfilment was not shared by his wife, Caroline. She resented what was going on, a resentment that expressed itself for a period of weeks personally against Colin: 'She wanted nothing to do with me and hated the thought of me even touching her. There was hardly any communication between us. Instead of growing together in the Spirit, we were growing apart.' Family life was so fraught that one day Caroline said, 'If I had anywhere to go with the children, I would walk out and leave you.' In spite of the evident tension she did not walk out and, later, as we shall see, came to experience the blessings that characterised the life of St Hugh's.

Widening circles

It was inevitable that the unusual and exciting events at St Hugh's should have attracted outside attention. The evening services were attended by scores of people from other churches, drawn to St Hugh's by the accounts that filtered through of the Holy Spirit's life-changing power. The whole spectrum of Christianity in Britain was represented at those services: Brethren, Baptist, Methodist, Anglican, Roman Catholic, to name but a few, all eager to discover what had caused the change at St Hugh's. Renewal at the church thus spilled over into the other denominations, a most welcome development as far as Colin was concerned, then as now. People were touched by God and went back to their own churches revitalised and with a fresh vision for God's work. Another indication that St Hugh's was attracting outside attention was the fact that well-known visitors came to the parish, either to observe what was going on or to preach. Colin began to receive invitations to preach elsewhere, conducting a weekend for young people in a church near Brighton, a 'New Life' conference in Southport, and a healing conference in Cardiff. Here were foretastes of his later travelling ministry.

Setbacks

As well as the attention, there were difficulties and sadnesses too. In May 1973, an arson attack was made on the church building. The following morning when Colin went into the church to prepare for Holy Communion, he was met by a thick wall of smoke. As he opened the door the smoke rushed out causing him to stagger back. This is what happened next, in Colin's own words:

> I could see flames just inside the door, so I ran into the church hall for water and managed to put that fire out. I could hear crackling noises coming from the direction of the altar at the other end of the building. The smoke was so dense that I could only take a few steps before being driven back. I rang for the fire brigade.[10]

The police arrived, followed by the local fire chief who stood in the church shaking his head in disbelief: he simply could not understand why the whole building had not gone up in smoke, declaring, 'A building with this volume of air should have burned easily.' He explained this on perfectly reasonable natural grounds, but the church, and Colin, would have put forward another and very different explanation: the guarding providence of God protecting the building for His work.

Even more distressing was the death of Gomer, whose baptism in the Holy Spirit had been significant in the renewal process in the church, and who had a real vision of the way God wanted to work amongst the church as a family. Soon after his re-election as a churchwarden, he was diagnosed as having sciatica, but further tests indicated that the trouble was in fact a brain tumour. Five weeks later he died in hospital. His death affected Colin deeply and personally as he and Gomer had become friends as well as being involved in the life of St Hugh's. Throughout the period of Gomer's hospitalisation and subsequent death, God taught the congregation a number of important lessons which are as relevant today as they were almost twenty years ago.

The first lesson was that Gomer was a son of God and that his life belonged to God his heavenly father.

The second lesson was the need to prepare people for death while continuing to pray for healing. Gomer was treated with dignity and compassion, with no attempt to disguise the seriousness of his illness from him or to live in unreality. Colin said to him one day:

> 'When you die, I shall be the most jealous man in Lewsey.'
> I had experienced a taste of heaven, and I knew what I was talking about. Gomer was already at one with the Lord – so there was nothing to fear in dying! To the last, he remained a great witness to the hospital staff. He could be a very impatient man, but throughout his illness he was filled with the patience that is a precious fruit of the Holy Spirit.[11]

The third lesson was that Gomer's illness had to be viewed within the context of the entire church:

> We called the church family to a day of prayer with fasting. It was another sign of love, that the whole family responded to this, even though fasting was a new experience for many. We did not pray only for Gomer; we knew that, as a body, we needed to learn all the lessons the Lord was wanting to teach us through this situation.
>
> Through Gomer's illness we were moving further towards what the Lord wanted us to be; a body of people bound together in love. Many of those who had argued against this life of commitment to one another now found themselves doing it quite naturally. But at what a cost!
>
> Gomer continued to grow weaker. He was dying. I knew it. He knew it.[12]

The fourth lesson was that difficult questions arising out of a death like Gomer's *have* to be faced. Only thus can a church body retain its integrity in the face of apparent tragedy. Colin's comment on the significance of Gomer's illness and subsequent death deserves to be spelled out at length:

> Where was the power of Jesus in His Body at St Hugh's? We were used to people being healed, not dying. Could we have done anything more to prevent his death? We had prayed, we had fasted and listened to the Lord. It seemed that even in Gomer's death we were being taught. The Lord had chosen to raise His son to glory and he had given us all a sense of that glory as we gave thanks for our brother. We had acknowledged that God had the right to do whatever He pleased with His son.
>
> If we could say, 'Lord fulfil your perfect will for Gomer,' should we not also be praying, 'Lord do whatever you like with each one of us, so that you may use all of us for your purpose'? Or, were we all to wait until our deathbeds before we would be prepared to recognise God's sovereign authority in our own lives?

This word 'authority' came to the forefront of our life at St Hugh's, together with the words 'rebellion' and 'obedience'.

Were we prepared to recognise the Lord's authority in our lives? If so, we needed to repent of all the rebellion against Him that still existed within us. We had to go through a period of deep introspection.

The Lord showed us that, individually, selfish desires still dominated parts of our lives. Many of us were still 'conformed to this world', and all of us needed to be further transformed by the renewal of our minds (see Romans 12:2).

For a few weeks, it was difficult to praise the Lord together; even our worship seemed 'heavy'. Whenever we wanted to relax and rejoice in the Lord, He prevented us, and made us look at ourselves. No wonder! We were disobedient children and our Father was confronting us with our disobedience . . .

When the Lord touches someone on a raw spot, there is a natural tendency to project what He is saying on to other people, which can make us critical of them. It is easy to acknowledge God's words when He is saying pleasant things; not so easy when He is shining His light into the dark recesses of our lives, revealing areas of disobedience to His Word.

The Lord showed us that if we were not prepared to accept the authority of the Word of God, and the leading of the Spirit within the Body of Christ, then we were rebelling against Him. He had placed His authority within the Body of Christ. As members of His Body we could not regard ourselves as free agents to do as we pleased. If we were committed to the Lord we were committed to a new way of life, centred upon Him.

It is one thing to be grateful that He has given us new life, it is another thing to hear Him saying that this leads to a new way of living. Some did not want to hear this, yet at every turn this was clearly what God was saying. A good deal of criticism was directed towards me . . .

It was not until after Gomer's death that we began to see the seriousness of such thinking. This was not discontent with me; it was discontent with God Himself and the way that He was leading us. This was rebellion against the purpose of Almighty God. I began to appreciate this, so did some others, but how could the situation be remedied? I could hardly stand up in the pulpit and say: 'Some of you are feeling rebellious towards me and that means you are rebelling against the Lord.' Some would miss the point completely and accuse me of thinking that only I was being led by the Spirit![13]

Put simply: God's sovereignty is a truth that has to be accepted, whatever the cost, whatever the pain involved in the situation. A corollary is that no amount of bluster can obscure the fact that God is the healer, and that sometimes people are not healed despite all the prayer and faith in the world. A case like Gomer's highlights man's limitations in the face of the problem of pain and suffering. Hard lessons are as important in spiritual development as the stories of success and miraculous healing, and this is what the congregation at St Hugh's came to discern and accept.

A transformed congregation : the reasons

During his time at Luton Colin was privileged to lead the church into renewal and revival, characterised by miracles of healing, a full-orbed demonstration of the gifts of the Spirit, including speaking in tongues and words of knowledge, and vigorous and varied praise and worship, but perhaps above all by love. Anointed and powerful preaching contributed to the equally important growth in spiritual maturity and all-round understanding of God's purposes in the lives of believers. A perfectly ordinary, run-of-the-mill Anglican church was changed beyond recognition within a comparatively short space of time, five years in all. Not all the changes were to the liking of every member – this could scarcely be possible – but the majority of the parishioners undoubtedly responded positively, if fearfully at times, to the manifest leading of the Holy Spirit in worship, preaching and life-style.

What then explains these events at St Hugh's church?

Freshness

One factor contributing to the transformation of St Hugh's may have been the freshness and openness of Colin's response to renewal, amounting to what might be called naivety. This word is not used perjoratively. Colin had an uncluttered acceptance of the Word of God as guided by the Holy Spirit, and it is something Charles Sibthorpe noticed later at The Hyde: 'There was almost a naive response from Colin when he discovered a new truth in the Bible. If he found a new truth at nine thirty he would expect to put it into practice *immediately*.' Colin would not agonise about the freshly discovered emphasis in the Word of God; he would at once see it as normative for his life and for those around him. There was no attempt to conceptualise the ideas, simply to put them into the context of faith and daily living at once. More conservatively-minded leaders might well ponder the likely effect of such revelations on their congregations, whereas Colin sought to utilise them, with immediate effect:

> We were not a very old church, but we needed to be renewed in love. We could not choose the way to be renewed; only the Lord could do that. He wanted to baptise us in the Holy Spirit; we allowed him to do so. He wanted to share with us the gifts of the Holy Spirit; we gratefully accepted them and it is certain that the renewal of our church would not be taking place without the use of these gifts. He wanted to lead us into a new commitment to one another in love so that the world around us might believe; after some rebellion we are allowing Him to do that now.[14]

Willingness and obedience

Colin's willingness to allow the Spirit to operate freely and sovereignly was another factor in the transformation of the Church. It extended to a willingness to review traditional patterns and structures within the local church:

> There are so many weighty decisions requiring spiritual rather than practical insight. As we recognised our need in this direction and prayed about it, so the Lord began to raise up lay people who could share in the spiritual responsibilities of our church family. Again, these have needed to be those who would make their lives available to the Lord, so that they can be 'the willing servants of all'.[15]

The centrality of the Bible

As led by Colin, the church came to the convinction that the Bible is to be read, believed and acted upon. This constituted *the* standard or guideline by which the members of St Hugh's were to assess their behaviour and regulate their lives. They did not regard themselves as free to act in whatever way they liked; they accepted the authority of the Scriptures and the leading of the Spirit on a personal and corporate level.

Prayer

The importance of prayer was linked directly by Colin to the practice of meditation and of listening daily to God's directives. At several key points in his ministry at St Hugh's, Colin received a personal word relating to his life and that of the church. Here the distinction is between Scripture (God's direct and objective Word) and the prophetic word (God's indirect word). During

Lent 1971, as the church thought deeply about the place of healing in its life and witness, they were given a prophecy which said:

> Turn to me and you will be filled with joy and your healing will be assured, for I am the Lord who cares for you and you are my people whom I shall always love. So come to me and share in the inheritance that is yours – healing and wholeness. This is my gift for those who repent, that they will know that I am their God. They will know that they can turn to me in their sickness and they will be healed.
>
> But those who have not turned to me with their whole heart, they do not know; they do not claim the assurance I offer them. There is only one way to receive my gifts – come to me in sorrow for what you have become and I will make you glad in what you should be – more, I will pour my gifts into your heart and make you mine forever.
>
> Rejoice my people, for the day of your deliverance has come. Turn and be healed, for I would fill you with myself. My people, I love you. Will you spurn my love? Will you turn away from I who am your health? My people, I am your healing and your health, turn to me and be restored. Be made whole and you will live to my glory and be happy.[16]

This prophecy increased the faith of the members, and encouraged them to pray for healing for colds, acne, catarrh, among other things – small healings in other words; but it also taught them that healing cannot be divorced or isolated from the rest of the gospel. In this way St Hugh's began to experience what the New Testament calls 'signs following', that is, particular evidences of God's power, be it in healing, words of knowledge, the gift of faith, and so on.

Gentleness

Another characterstic of the transformation of St Hugh's was gentleness in the management of change. Great care was taken in the leading of people into the experience of God, particularly into the baptism of the Holy Spirit.

Children

Right from the commencement of Colin's ministry in Luton, children were viewed as important to the overall success of the church. *When the Spirit Comes* records how many children experienced healings, exercised the gifts of the Spirit, including speaking in tongues, were taught how to relate to each other, and how to enjoy a natural relationship with the Lord Jesus. They also played their part in the praise and worship at the church. No mere appendages to what was occurring in the lives of their parents and grandparents, they were treated with respect and dignity.

This is what happened to one of Colin and Caroline's own children, Claire, one Sunday evening:

> Claire and Clive had just gone to bed. Claire was then six years old and Clive, four.
>
> 'Go up and kiss the children goodnight,' Caroline called out as I came in.
>
> As I entered the bedroom the two children shared, I heard Clive ask: 'Where is Jesus?'
>
> 'He's alive inside us. Didn't you know that, silly?' Claire answered. Just like an elder sister! 'That's right isn't it, Dad?' she asked as I walked up to her bed.
>
> 'Yes, that's right,' I said.
>
> 'Can Jesus live in me?' asked Claire.
>
> 'Yes, He can live in anyone who wants Him.'
>
> 'How?'
>
> Ah! Now I knew the answer!

'Tell the Lord you want to give Him your life and ask Him to come and live in you,' I said.

Immediately, Claire knelt on top of her bed, closed her eyes and put her hands together, in good Sunday School style. 'Please Jesus, come and live in me,' she prayed.

She looked happy.

'I want you to pray again,' I told her; 'this time, let Jesus give you the words to say.'

She prayed for all the people in the world who do not know the Lord, that they might come to see His glory. Hardly the prayer of a six-year-old.

Dad was happy! – and I expect our heavenly Father was smiling too!

'Now then, come along, it's time you tucked down and went to sleep,' I said to them both.

'Wait a minute, Daddy, I haven't said my other prayer,' protested Claire.

'What other prayer?'

She began to speak in tongues![17]

Love

Colin consistently taught that without love, Christians are merely empty vessels, making noises but not much else. If St Hugh's was to be an example to the outside world, love had to operate within the church first. It began with repentance and forgiveness. Love was particularly powerfully demonstrated when Gomer was dying with cancer, and eventually led to this direct word to Colin:

> You are to commit your lives to me – to be led by my Holy Spirit.

You are to promise obedience to the leading of my Spirit within the Community.

You are to worship and pray together in the Spirit.

You are to love one another – have that relationship with one another that is pleasing to me.

You are to be concerned with the spreading of my Word of Truth in this parish.

You are to show the quality of love I require of my children to Christians of other churches.

I, the Lord, promise to lead you in all things – to enrich greatly your lives with many blessings, if you will only be faithful to me in this. I will enter into an agreement with you, an agreement which I will honour because of my love for you. Let no one be afraid of entering into an agreement with me, for by doing this you will be bound closer to me in love.[18]

Here was an outline, a blueprint for the life of the church there: commitment, obedience, worship, prayer, love, evangelism and witness. For some in the church, including Colin and Caroline, it meant living together in community, a demanding way of life for all involved.

Relationships

From the very beginning of his ministry, Colin taught that relationships between the members of the church were meant to reflect the relationship between Jesus and His Father, and between Jesus and His Church. *My Father is the Gardener* began as a teaching book on John chapter 15 with its central picture of the vine tree, with its interrelated branches: security in identity and unity. Colin realised that if the church was to prosper, its relationships had to be on a right and just footing, with people caring for each other in honesty, integrity and, above all, in love, 'agape' love as signally shown by our Lord.

Personal example

Another facter in the transformation of the church was Colin's willingness to follow God obediently in his own personal life, and to lead his congregation where he himself had gone. For him, the journey of discovery at St Hugh's was from revelation, via repentance, to renewal. Colin believed that those in spiritual leadership must first be the living expression of God's life and power, being obedient to the teaching of the Scriptures and reaching out with the resources they themselves have received from God. Only as the leaders of churches are themselves continually receiving revelation, continually being repentant, and continually being renewed will their congregations proceed along the same route. Of course this brand of leadership involves sensitivity to the Holy Spirit who 'gives the anointing that will encourage others to follow. Leadership includes setting the right example, not driving people.'[19] And the cardinal principle is that each leader or group of leaders must discover for themselves what God is saying in relation to their congregations, not aping what has happened in other churches.

The whole process, as Colin found at Luton, is costly, requiring discipline, dedication and not a little patience. It is costly, too, in terms of time and energy, but nothing is more exciting than seeing God at work in a congregation, transforming it so fundamentally that it becomes the body of Christ in its locality, reaching out to the poor and needy with the life and power of Jesus, with His love and joy and peace, with His forgiveness and healing.

4

ST HUGH'S UNDER SCRUTINY

Quite clearly Colin's spiritual world at Luton was one that he had not known before. He experienced things daily that he didn't know were possible, and one of the most important of these was the 'ability to hear God speak clearly', which is as prominent a feature of his ministry today as it was in those heady days of twenty years ago.

Colin's perception of his time at St Hugh's, Lewsey is summed up in chapter one of *Faith For The Future*.[1] There are several different aspects to it. One is that God 'accomplished a sovereign work' there, which was a 'great encouragement to many other churches'. Another is that there was a considerable 'increase in my heart for both God and people, and also a new note of authority that had not been present in my ministry previously'. Then, 'People were meeting with Jesus personally as never before.' This stress on an encounter or meeting with God is as characteristic of his ministry today as it was then at the start of the nineteen seventies.

These were – and are – Colin's judgements, but how did others assess his work and influence at Lewsey? 'Colin did a remarkable work at St Hugh's, Lewsey', said Lord Runcie,[2] formerly Archbishop of Canterbury but at that time Colin's Bishop, 'pursuing a sacrificial ministry which drew to him a number of disciples and they created a congregation of formidable shape and generosity.' He adds: 'But of course it was at some cost to his own personal and domestic life as well as the parish.'

Where renewal sweeps through a church, particularly an Anglican church with desires for a quiet life, there is inevitably an upheaval. Conflict can only be expected in such circumstances, and St Hugh's was no exception.

It was not easy for those desiring an easy life to hear about a living and personal relationship with Jesus; for them Colin's teaching must have been threatening in the extreme. Such people wanted an undisturbed, and undemanding faith which was dusted down once a week on Sundays. Nor can it have been easy for some members of the congregation to be confronted by a Vicar who, though an Anglican priest, seemed very 'un-Anglican' in some of his attitudes and teaching. He clearly did not want to run his parish on typically 'safe' lines; rather he wanted to bring his congregation under the dynamite of the Holy Spirit's life and influence.

The wider scene

The significance of Colin's time in Luton was considerable, not least because of the Church's part in the wider charismatic movement. At the outset, neither Colin nor the congregation had any idea of events taking place in the wider Christian world. There was, for Colin, none of the agonising controversy that seems to have plagued David Watson, for example, following his baptism in the Holy Spirit. As Canon Watson's biographers, Teddy Saunders and Hugh Sansom show, his experience was both joyful, because of the unmistakeable release of God's life and joy into his soul, and perplexing because of theological and personal ramifications. David Watson eventually concluded that 'the baptism in the Holy Spirit refers to Christian initiation. It is the spiritual event by which all people are brought into the

Christ, whether Jews or Gentiles.'³ Personally he encountered considerable opposition, even to the extent of being turned out of his lodgings in Tyndale House in Cambridge because the authorities there had heard that he used tongues privately in his prayers.

Unlike David Watson, Colin was not constrained when it came to taking his church in the direction he felt God wanted: nothing else mattered to him, then, or now. Unlike David Watson, too, Colin had no links with the public school element (E. J. Nash's Iwerne camps in particular) which tended to require a group response, even group conformity, on matters of theological belief and style. Again this freedom was advantageous.

The renewal at St Hugh's attracted the attention not only of other churches, but of publishers, too. One visitor to Luton in 1973 was Edward England, later the editor of *Renewal* but at that time working for Hodder & Stoughton. His visit was prompted by three separate friends who had heard Colin preach. He recalls:

As I sat in Colin's study I glanced, as I always do, at his library. Not only were there few books but those that were there were not reassuring. With the exception of *The Normal Christian Life*, by Watchman Nee, the reading of which had changed his life, most of the classic preacher's books were missing from his shelves. His books certainly did not represent evangelical scholarship or the charismatic viewpoint which I expected. If he wasn't a reader, was he a writer? In his vicarage I invited him to write a book about his experience of the Holy Spirit. I did so hesitantly. He appeared to know more about cricket than writing. The modest advance I offered for his first book reflected my doubts. I advised that he submitted the first chapters for comment, and this he did. Inevitably they needed editing but the material was dynamic. At that stage I had no idea that Colin would become one of the biggest-selling Christian authors, whose books would be sought after by many publishers.⁴

Edward England launched *When the Spirit Comes* the following year. Six years later, Colin was among the first authors to join Edward's literary agency when he left Hodder & Stoughton. Edward wrote to him on August 21st, 1980, at that time intending to limit himself to fifty authors: 'Welcome to the Fifty Club. It means a great deal to me to include what my wife Ann describes as "three men of the Spirit", David Watson, Michael Harper and yourself, also because our association goes back a long way.'

Colin's time at St Hugh's also launched him on an international ministry. Many hundreds of people all over the world were being converted under Colin's preaching and many others experiencing real spiritual life for the first time. Lord Runcie believes that St Hugh's, Lewsey was the cradle in which Colin was born as a world evangelist, and he comments:

> Like John Wesley he began to take the world for his parish; but equally like John Wesley he was not prepared to give time to the half-hearted, not very religious, semi-believers who needed pastoral care in the parish.
>
> I don't think Colin's ministry was very effective amongst the more intelligent and sophisticated; but then, 'not many wise, not many learned' . . . It was also one that seriously divided the local community and also separated him from the fellowship of local clergy.
>
> I have an affection and admiration for Colin. He could be a threat to Bishops and conventional parish priests. He was not prepared to make the inevitable compromises demanded by a parish ministry in England. But within that ministry God was calling him to other work.

This assessment accords with that of several other observers at the time. It also accords with the certainty God gave Colin that his voice would be heard among the nations, not just within the confines of a parish church. Indeed, given the quite specific word Colin had heard from God, that his voice would extend throughout the world, it was inevitable that, one day, he would venture forth into a wider sphere of work and influence.

One country in which Colin's voice has been heard consistently over the ensuing years is Australia. In that country he has forged a close working relationship and friendship with Harry Westcott, chairman of Vision Ministries, who recalls his first encounter with Colin in the early nineteen seventies:[5]

> My first impression of his preaching was like that I had never heard before. Our phrase is, 'he's a hand of iron in a velvet glove'. His English accent allowed him to say incredibly bold things, including statements of rebuke, and we all sat there and 'amended' our judgements. His arrival at my parish, O'Connor Methodist Church in Canberra, found our church going through a very similar move of the Spirit that he had earlier experienced at St Hugh's. The Holy Spirit fell on our church in early 1974 and Colin came to us first when we needed guidance and good solid teaching in the Word. So over the next few years he became an apostle to both the church and myself, its pastor.

In 1976, Colin again visited Westcott's church:

> I remember on that occasion the kind of directness that typifies Colin's assurance as a Christian leader. He came to the church which was packed to crushing point, we believed we had matured and were now strong charismatic Methodists, and as the pastor I was proud of the church's growth and strength. After the meeting we were having our evening coffee together in the Manse and Colin (as usual) was fairly quiet and non-committal. I said to him with a great deal of pride, 'Well, Colin, what do you think of the church?' He replied: 'Have you got that prayer counselling thing going in this church?' I said, 'You bet we have, we're up to our eyeballs in it, it's the greatest discovery for ministering to a congregation I've ever experienced.' He then flattened me with this statement: 'Well, get rid of it, it will kill faith in the people.' With open mouth I retired to my study seeking strength to fight another day. All I know is that from that day I stopped looking back, back, back at the problems of life and began appropriating the glorious Word of God by faith. It set me free.

Westcott comments further on that visit of 1976:

> That experience typified for me Colin's complete confidence
> in the Word of God and his distrust of all that is worldly in
> setting people free. His preaching is uncompromising in the
> whole area of faith and it is refreshing as we in Australia have
> been bombarded by so much American hype and razzmataz.
> The Americans come preaching faith with all the glitter that
> money can buy. They have to have the best hotels, the best
> cars, wear the best suits, and desire the best hospitality.
> However, Colin came preaching Christ, looked like he slept
> in his trousers, didn't demand hotel accommodation, and
> never talked money. But he *lived faith*, and his ministry
> has proved that in the material things of life he is more
> successful and more affluent than many of his American
> counterparts.

A leader with vision

Colin's ability to impart a vision to St Hugh's must not be
overlooked when considering the significance of his ministry.
He gave St Hugh's a basis for a church prepared to move
forward. His distinctly iconoclastic ministry facilitated this.
Colin freed the church from simply existing and 'doing the
rounds' of church affairs. He taught that there was much more
to church life than merely activities and functions. He led his
congregation into viewing what went on in the church as part
of God's purpose for bringing in kingdom life and kingdom
power. In this sense, therefore, he had a vision for St Hugh's
which wasn't mere survival as a conventional parish church.
While some have criticised Colin for a failure to construct
pastoral structures to cope with the renewed life and vigour,
there can be no minimising of the vision itself, which he taught
consistently and also embodied in his running of the parish.

For Colin himself, the time at St Hugh's gave him a growing

personal confidence. This was not pride or overweening confidence, rather a genuine belief that he could lead people to God, and that he really did hear from God. An example of the fruit of this listening is the bestselling *My Dear Child*, the product of a lifetime's listening. Colin listened to God *for* the people, a sort of inspired spiritual intermediary. This capacity and willingness to listen to God for large tracts of time gives Colin's ministry a strength and quality often lacking in the ministry of many well-known speakers.

St Hugh's under Colin's leadership was changed radically in all aspects of its life: in worship, in response to the Word of God, in its reception of the gifts of the Spirit and the ministry of healing, in terms of personal piety and devotion to God. One person, however, continued to be largely unaffected by the excitement and thrill of renewal. That person was Colin's wife, Caroline.

5

'WHERE ARE YOU, COLIN?'

Caroline Urquhart, a gentle, undemonstrative woman, has told her story in *His God, My God*, published in 1983. It became a best-seller, one of the reasons for its success being her honesty and directness. There was no attempt to obscure the difficulties and heartache that arose for her and the family because Colin was so committed to the work at St Hugh's. Nor was there any subterfuge in portraying herself self-pityingly as the injured party who got everything right whereas Colin got it wrong. She strikes the right balance between fact and interpretation, between honesty and loyalty. She told an ordinary story, in many ways, with dignity and composure, and one suspects that telling her story was probably the last thing she wanted to do, as she does not court publicity. She is perfectly content to support Colin in his work for God, to be, in scriptural terms, a 'helper' to him, making sure that he is able to fulfil his ministry in the most successful manner possible. Her unpretentiousness, ordinariness and genuine integrity impressed readers in their thousands.

His God, My God cuts through to the heart of a perennial temptation for those involved in full-time ministry: to neglect the life of the family because the work of God is coming along so well. Few callings are as potentially corrosive of home life as full-time Christian ministry, and many men would profit from a careful reading of what Caroline has to say, the more so because she says it so affably and temperately.

The realities of the Urquhart family situation were simple enough. Looking after Claire, Clive and Andrea was a demanding task, and the house Caroline had to look after was bigger than anything she had lived in before. Constant tiredness was allied to a crippling sense of inadequacy and inability to cope. The wonder is that she coped so well under the circumstances.

She felt trapped, and paralysed by a feeling of 'hopelessness' (her description). Her horizons were strictly limited. Her world was bounded by the children, with their constant need of attention and care, by the expectations of the parish, and by her settled conviction that she was a failure. She thus had no long-term plans or strategies; all she wanted to do was 'survive a few hours at a time'. Her feelings were exacerbated because Colin was clearly so fruitfully occupied with extending God's kingdom while she felt defeated.

Caroline was clear about one thing: she did not want to be involved in the life of the parish, whatever the expectations placed upon her by other people. Equally clearly, she did not want to know about the renewal going on at St Hugh's. She was in the minority of those who were not changing with the wind of renewal sweeping through the church. In fact, she was frightened when she observed other people being healed, drawn into a new relationship with God, being free in praise and worship, and thus giving all the indications of living on a different spiritual plane to herself.

Amidst all the clutter of home and the frenetic activity going on around her at church, Caroline felt lonely and isolated:

> As I fussed around in the kitchen doing nothing, I was aware that Colin was sitting quietly. Goodness knows what he was thinking. At last he got up heavily and went to the study to collect something for the afternoon. A few moments later he called out. 'See you, darling. Have a good time.' The door closed and I was alone again.
>
> As soon as he had passed the kitchen window, I leant against

the table and closed my eyes, squeezing them tight to hold
back the tears.

'Have a good time,' he said.[1]

Eventually her attitude turned to one of resentment. Positive
things were happening to other people, they were finding peace
and joy in their lives while she was in a depressing turmoil.
Caroline oscillated between wanting to be part of renewal
and not wanting to be involved at all. She was frightened
and uncertain about her future position and rôle in the renewal
process going on at St Hugh's.

She felt a spiritual failure. She wasn't even sure that God
existed, let alone was someone who answers prayers. To
her, Colin's eager and enthusiastic talk about God affecting
everyday lives and situations seemed remote, far-fetched, even
esoteric to a person like herself who was, as she readily admits,
woefully ignorant about the Bible and who God was supposed
to be. Colin's sermons did not help much either because, with
the children to control, it was difficult to concentrate for herself.
She went, for the most part, out of sheer duty, slipping in just
before the service started. How could she possibly move into
renewal when her own relationship with God was so tenuous
and fragile?

The challenge of others

Yet there were certain facts she could not deny. Andrea's
healing was the first. The intimacy of Colin's relationship with
God was a second. Third, he had changed radically in outlook,
belief and behaviour though not, it seems, towards her.

For the moment her response to this evidence was muted,
and she concentrated on surviving. For approximately eighteen
months at St Hugh's, Caroline simply ignored those aspects of
Colin's ministry that she found uncongenial or too challenging.

55

One facet of life at St Hugh's was particularly threatening to her: the baptism in the Holy Spirit. With self-deprecating humility, she assumed that such an experience was the preserve of the super-charged, super-spiritual people, far removed from herself and her very limited awareness of God and His power.

In this she was, of course, misguided, but what happened to two local people, David and Jane, gave her much cause for thought. Not being members of the church, they had originally booked the church hall for their wedding reception, the intention being to hold the church service elsewhere. These plans were changed when they realised the modern church would also be convenient for the service, too. As one of them lived within the parish boundaries, this was possible, but Colin had a further stipulation: that couples he married had either to attend a marriage preparation course or a 'Know Jesus' series. David and Jane agreed, and at the end of the teaching time Colin asked them if they wanted to know Jesus for themselves: 'This they did, and on their final visit, ten days before the wedding, they both together asked Jesus to come into their lives and fill them with His Holy Spirit. Evidently He did. You could see the joy shining from them at this heavenly wedding present.'[2]

Caroline was overwhelmed. Her defences were lowered even more by the conversion of their eldest child, Claire. One night as Colin came downstairs from putting the children to bed his eyes were joyful yet cautious. He told Caroline that 'Claire had asked Jesus into her life and had prayed in tongues.' She was only six years old. Caroline describes her response like this:

> After a long discussion one night, Colin asked me if I would like him to pray with me to be filled with the Spirit. I decided I would. I knew enough about it, and was intrigued. It might solve all my problems and bring me closer to Colin.

> We knelt together on the carpet. I felt clumsy and awkward, but being on my knees helped to arrange my thoughts into a suitable mood. My heart was beating fast and my face felt flushed. Was this it?

Colin prayed a very simple prayer in English. I said 'Amen' and fully intended to pray myself, but was choked and couldn't. After a pause, Colin placed his hands on my head and prayed in tongues aloud for several minutes. The floor was hard under my knees and sitting on my shoes wasn't comfortable after a while. I wriggled a bit. Colin paused and caught my eye. My high hopes, which had been faltering, were now completely dashed. Determinedly Colin prayed again.

'Father, we thank You for hearing our prayers and leading us up to this point. Continue to guide us both together in Your way. Amen.'[3]

Colin's prayer was not answered immediately. It did, though, become obvious to Caroline that the issue of baptism in the Spirit could not be ignored for ever. Influenced by gentle, unthreatening teaching by Colin on the love of God, she saw the various ways she had shunned God, and rejected His plans and benevolent care for her as a person, as an individual. Caroline now saw herself as a sinner, for whom Jesus died on the cross.

Encouragements

Many months later Colin received a prophetic word which concerned his wife:

Concerning your wife: know that she is as a bright jewel in My crown. Her sincerity of heart delights Me and I shall use her to point the way for many to My Kingdom. Your prayer to be united in My love has been heard and I make you this promise: As you remain faithful to Me, so shall I remain faithful to you, and your love for one another shall deepen, for the Son of Righteousness shall fill your life together. As the sun draws out the different colours of creation, so shall the Son highlight your love for one another. You have much to learn together but I will be your teacher . . .[4]

A further important piece in the jigsaw was Caroline's acceptance that her own resources were not adequate; they were finite and limited, and rather dramatically one day she flung herself on the bed, devoid of strength, of will-power, at the end of her own resources. She cried, 'God, if you're there, you've got to help me. Show yourself to me.' She could not take any more. An enormous weight had fallen off her shoulders: she had found peace. This was a quantum leap for her; it was the beginning of her journey to real faith and real confidence in God.

Imperceptibly, but quite definitely, Caroline's life and attitudes changed. She gained control, to a greater measure than ever before, over those negative thoughts which had so embittered her relationships previously. She began to recognise that her inferiority complex had hardened into pride, the 'great sin' according to C. S. Lewis. She found she could accept that life without Jesus Christ at the helm is a wretched and unsatisfactory affair, and became more open to receiving God's help and peace. Gradually, she grew in confidence regarding her place in the total life of the parish; she began to gain a sense of purpose and identity – that is, her own identity, not simply in relation to Colin.

The outward circumstances of her life remained much the same throughout these personal and largely inner changes: a hectic life-style, the constant demands of the children, strained resources of space and finances. But now Caroline and Colin faced the situations together and together found God's strength and comfort.

After working through her pain and resentment, Caroline emerged a stronger person, a more resolute Christian altogether. Looking back to those difficult days, she is absolutely convinced that there always was a link with God in her life, although she did not know Him. It is clear, too, that Satan exploited areas of insecurity and weakness in her life. Owing to the fact that her mother left home when Caroline was very young, she had no rôle model to copy, no one whose experience and wisdom she could fall back on when domestic problems occurred. This missing dimension in her life, allied to her feelings of failure, contrived to make her feel inadequate – and this at a time when her husband was frantically busy with a 'successful' parish; of course, his success made her feel more desperate than she might have had she possessed a strong sense of her own self-worth. Her ignorance of the Bible did not help either, because she had no framework of knowledge as a resource. The temptation to fall back on Colin's faith must have been considerable, but in the end she forged her own relationship with God in a way that has stood the test of time.

Today Caroline is still not the sort of person to broadcast her Christian views, still less her virtues, but she is manifestly a strong, dependable Christian who is probably at her best in talking to individuals, counselling, advising and being herself. Her support is absolutely vital to Colin as he seeks to lead Roffey Place into a new period of fruitfulness and blessing.

6

LEAVING ST HUGH'S

Early in his ministry at St Hugh's, Colin had received a specific promise from God: 'Your voice must be heard among the nations, and if you do not speak my people will not hear.' His initial response was one of sheer disbelief, and instinctively he wanted to reject the very idea of a travelling international ministry. At the time he was totally unaware of a global move of the Holy Spirit. He had no other ambition than to be a faithful parish priest. But the promise remained in the background of his thinking throughout the exciting, busy and extremely rewarding years from 1970 onwards.

The success of Colin's ministry meant that he began to receive an increasing number of invitations to preach and minister elsewhere: at conferences, parish weekends, mid-week prayer meetings, Sunday services, and so on. When his account of renewal at St Hugh's, *When the Spirit Comes*, was published in November 1974, the trickle of invitations to speak became a veritable flood.

Colin now had to face the possibility that God was calling him to move away from St Hugh's, a prospect he faced calmly and without fuss. On All Saints Day 1974, God reminded him of the promise and told him, more specifically, that it was now time to move out into a wider ministry. Alongside this word from God was Colin's increasing feeling of being 'at home' when addressing large conferences and assemblies. He knew that in such a way he was fulfilling the true ministry to which he had been called.

In spite of this conviction, and the very definite, quite unmistakeable word from God, leaving St Hugh's was not easy. Caroline was appalled by the thought of leaving the church, although she had known for some time that, eventually, they would have to move on, 'but surely not yet'. She had personal reasons for remaining in Luton: 'I was only just beginning to grow as a Christian, and the thought of living without the parish community seemed impossible.' Both Colin and Caroline, however, knew that God's will was for them to leave, and this inner conviction quelled any other hesitations they may have had.

Certain official and legal formalities were processed, together with a visit to the Bishop, Robert Runcie, who assured Colin of his prayerful support at all times. Eventually the Deed of Resignation was signed, making their decision irrevocable. Although he was not leaving the Church of England, Colin was now without a parish, and from now on they would, quite literally, need to rely on God entirely for their daily bread and general provision.

East Molesey

New Year's Day 1976 dawned cold and wintry. It was the day the Urquhart family moved to live in East Molesey, Surrey, in a house owned by the Fountain Trust (an agency for the stimulation of charismatic renewal amongst all denominations). To them all, the cold weather seemed symbolic of the difficulties and adjustments that lay ahead. Caroline notes two major areas of adjustment. The first was financial. No regular salary came in each month, and they seldom, if ever, had more than they needed to meet household bills, food, travelling expenses, etc. The timing of the incoming cheques and money, however, reminded them that God was a loving and caring heavenly Father. The second was administrative. Being totally unfamiliar with the planning of an itinerant ministry, the first few months were a little chaotic, the biggest temptation being to leave too little time between trips to sort out the correspondence and the long-term organisation.

There seemed very little time for relaxation of any sort, but help was at hand. Six months after moving to Surrey, the Urquharts came into contact with George and Hazel Hoerder. Not only did they live close by, but George was a retired Army Brigadier, well acquainted with administrative procedures, while his wife was, in Caroline's words, 'full of faith-building stories about the way the Lord was working'. It was decided that George would look after Colin's diary and generally plan his trips, both at home and abroad. He continued to fulfil this rôle until the Urquhart family moved to The Hyde in 1978, after which Charles Sibthorpe assumed this responsibility. George Hoerder recalls those days:

I met Colin at a Fountain Trust conference, and agreed to look after his administration and diary. I also travelled with Colin occasionally, for example, to America in 1979. I also worked in tandem with Michael Barling and Michael Harper in preparation for the 1978 Canterbury Conference. I have several distinct recollections of Colin at this time. He was easy to work with: unfussy, friendly and reasonable. He didn't flap, just got on with the job in hand. He didn't say a great deal, but was unfailingly helpful whenever he could be.

He was also a man of prayer who spent much time each day communing and listening to God's voice for direction, guidance and communication.

This closeness to God was the crucible in which his faith was forged and developed, and was the source of his strength in preaching, which I found stimulating and constructive. I would say he was a great preacher. This closeness to God also meant that he was not afraid of persecution.

Home and abroad

Colin's travelling ministry evolved quickly, and he began to lead large services all over the world. He recognised the change in emphasis as compared with his parish ministry in Luton, when he had the help of two other ordained clergymen and six full-time lay workers:

> When travelling I did not have such a ministering body of people. More expectancy was directed towards me personally. I resisted that with all my might. People's expectancy needed to be in the Lord; it was to Him they should be looking, not me. And I believed fundamentally in the ministry of the Body, without emphasis upon any individual or personality. In time God was to modify these views. He showed me that the Scriptures are the revelation of God working through particular personalities. He will not work through those motivated by pride; He promises to bring them low. The more broken and humbled a man is before God, the more God can use him, whether in a non-spectacular role as a faithful servant and witness, or in a more public ministry of evangelism and healing.[1]

In a very real sense his whole life became a preparation for the Lord to speak and act through him, and he spent many hours listening to God so that he developed the sort of sensitive spiritual ear that hears and knows His voice. He appreciated, too, that assurance and boldness could only come through a relationship built on prayer. He also taught that local churches can only become meaningful expressions of the body of Christ as they suffuse and immerse their activities in prayer.

During 1976 the bulk of Colin's ministry was in Britain, but he also travelled extensively abroad, thus fulfilling the God-given vision to be a voice to the nations. He visited New Zealand and Australia that year, returning to both countries in 1977 as well as preaching in South Africa, while in 1978 he conducted a notable series of meetings in Canada.

By 1978 it became clear that further expansion of Colin's ministry would depend on increasing his team, and after much prayer, discussion and waiting upon God for the 'right people', David and Jane Brown joined his ministry team. They had both been born again and filled with the Holy Spirit under Colin's preaching at St Hugh's. He had also conducted their wedding service in February 1972. During the five years that followed they had grown as Christians and as members of the church family at St Hugh's. They occasionally travelled with Colin on some of his ministry trips and David began to take a leadership rôle within the church.

In 1977, God spoke to them and said that they would live in a large house and be involved in ministering to other people. More specifically, they were told that this work would be fulfilled with Colin and his family. This was surprising because by this stage Colin had left Luton to develop his itinerant ministry and neither David nor Jane were in regular contact with him. However, when Colin was invited to speak at St Hugh's in the winter of 1977, David told him what he felt God had been saying. 'I knew that from the moment I left St Hugh's,' was Colin's reply. So, in August 1978, having sold their house in Dunstable and David having resigned his job with a local newspaper, they, together with their two children Joanna and Jeremy, joined Colin and his family. David began to travel with Colin not only in Britain, but also in Australia, France, Singapore, South Africa, Switzerland and Zimbabwe. As some of these trips were over four weeks long, they began to forge a special relationship which, says David, 'was given to us for the sake of the kingdom of God'.

This was a time of considerable learning for David. He says: 'Colin taught me how to pray for miracles, to preach, to counsel, and also to pray for individuals. He showed me how to walk by faith and receive miraculous provision for the ministry and for our families.'

David was thus involved with the smooth running of Colin's

team and trips, while at the same time gaining invaluable experience personally from observing a leader like Colin at work in different contexts and in various countries all over the world. The relationship between Colin and David, which the latter believes 'was of the Holy Spirit', was to be highly important as an embryo Christian community, then known as the Bethany Fellowship, grew and developed rapidly between 1978 and 1982.

7

THE HYDE

Amidst all the travelling and preaching in 1978 one need was paramount: the provision of a secure base for Colin, his family and several helpers from his time at St Hugh's. By July this need was pressing. As usual, when faced with difficult or uncertain situations, Colin immersed himself in prayer and fasting. Eventually he received what he had been waiting for: a clear and specific word from God. It said: 'When you leave this place (the house in East Molesey), you will need to take nothing with you.'

The next day he was off to attend the Pre-Lambeth Conference at the University of Kent in Canterbury, where he was to conduct a seminar with Bishop Festo Kivengere of Uganda on 'Renewal and Revival'. This was to be followed immediately by an open conference, with delegates flying in from all over the world. At that weekend conference the matter of Colin needing a house was raised. He tells his own story:

> Someone had heard from someone else, who had heard from someone else that there was a someone at the conference who had recently inherited a house and wanted it used for Christian purposes. The last links in the chain were Michael and Jeanne Harper.

> Michael and I established contact with Michael Warren and his wife Gillie. It transpired that about a year previously Michael's mother had died, leaving an estate in Sussex to his sister, Mary, and himself. The estate was managed on their

behalf, and they wanted the main house used for the Lord's purposes. Their first thought was to make it a Christian Conference Centre. The Lord had prevented that, telling them that he had some particular use for it. At the right time he would send the right people to them. Meanwhile they were to keep the place ready for use.[1]

That house was The Hyde. The Warrens did not want to make any hasty or potentially unwise decisions regarding the future use of The Hyde, nor did Colin and his family. Accordingly a decision was reached to meet the following Thursday at the property itself. During the next four days Colin became increasingly convinced that this was the answer to their housing dilemma. Within two hours of meeting at The Hyde an agreement was reached in principle between the Urquharts and the owners of the building.

Originally an eighteenth-century hunting lodge and later extended into a spacious country house in 1842, The Hyde was beautifully furnished, had generous-sized rooms and, significantly, everything was in place to the last teaspoon. Extensive grounds (twenty-eight acres) surrounded the house, half of them laid out as formal gardens. In a tangible and magnificent way God had given Colin and his family faith for the future. After completing the legal formalities, they moved into The Hyde in August 1978. Together, the Urquharts, and the Browns formed an embryo Christian community which prayed together, worked together and believed God for everything together. They shared joys, sorrows, finances in a manner reminiscent of the Acts of the Apostles.

The Bethany Fellowship

With the expansion of the work, it was now felt prudent to form a charitable trust which became known as the Bethany Fellowship. Bethany, it may be recalled, was the place where

Jesus's friends lived and where he enjoyed many hours of loving and happy fellowship. It was also the place where Lazarus was raised from the dead and it was from Bethany that Jesus ascended back to His father, to reign as King of glory. Each of these facts associated with Bethany was significant for Colin's burgeoning ministry. A true home is characterised by love and acceptance, a place where, in Malcolm Muggeridge's memorable phrase, 'children can retire from the hurts of the world'. In the years following 1978 scores of people were to come to The Hyde in search of love and acceptance, to be healed emotionally and physically, and to be recommissioned in God's service. The Hyde became a place where people discovered the miracle-working power of God, not as an engineered thing, but simply as a development from a personal relationship with God. Christians of all ages, and of all denominations, began to find their true fulfilment as they allowed the ascended Lord to reign in their lives, and countless numbers of people came to a new place of commitment to God at The Hyde. The title adopted for the travelling ministry was 'Kingdom Faith Ministries'.

As the work continued to grow, so too did the numbers of helpers. In January 1979, Ginny Cox, who had been trained as an opera singer, came to give much-needed help in a variety of ways. She joined the community at The Hyde because she felt it was a step God was asking of her. It was an act of obedience, following unmistakeable guidance from God. It was a considerable change in direction for her as she had spent many years, both at the Royal College of Music and in Rome, training to become an opera singer. She benefited enormously from her time at The Hyde in a number of different ways. Not least of these was the powerful influence Colin had on her life. She remembers him, first and foremost, as a 'man of God, of integrity and righteousness'. She says of him:

> Colin was a man of prayer, who would always pray about a matter before embarking on a particular plan of action.

69

He was not a man of impulse or precipitate action. He knew a great deal about waiting on God in patience and prayerfulness.

He had the courage to confront issues, but also the courage to implement God's vision, once he was sure what that vision was, either for his own life or for the Fellowship. He was generous in the life of the community. He was a servant, prepared to serve others, not least with such mundane tasks as washing up. Although a shy and naturally retiring man, he had a delightful sense of humour.

But what of the claim that Colin is a 'poor communicator with people'? Ginny contends:

My view is that all too often people had too high expectations of him in terms of the day-to-day life of the community. It is true that he often appeared to be silent and remote from the rest of the people, but then he did have a great deal to think about, and undoubtedly was caught up with what was on his mind. His particular ministry, too, made enormous demands upon him in that he was always alert to what God was saying to him, especially before a big meeting or rally when he wanted to impart to the people what God had given to him whilst in prayer and in listening to God.

Ginny was, and is, deeply grateful to Colin:

I learnt many lessons from him, including the need to live by faith and by the Word of God, not our feelings, to pray consistently and regularly, to trust God absolutely as Someone who never fails, the principles of the Kingdom, and to be prepared to serve others. I was privileged to see Colin dealing with a number of critical problems in the life of the Fellowship, and I was impressed by his willingness to *live out* the Bible in daily life. His attitude when confronted by the most complex issues was to ask: 'What can we learn from these issues?' and, 'What is the truth in this situation?' He also encouraged us to think the best of other people, and not to judge others too harshly or unkindly.

The fruit of Colin's life is to be seen in the lives of many thousands of men and women whose lives have been transformed by his preaching and by his example.

She concludes:

If I had to highlight one thing about Colin Urquhart it would be his determination to be obedient to the Word of God, whatever the cost. God was always first for Colin. He lived in revival himself and was able to lead others to live that way too, in quick forgiveness, and in behaviour watered by the love of God.

In August 1979, the community at The Hyde burgeoned with the arrival of twenty new people. One of those arrivals offers the following balanced assessment of the positive and negative features of Colin's influence:

There were three families plus several single people living in The Hyde at that time, which obviously created certain tensions. For instance, the parents of the three families held differing views on child-rearing, which meant that the children of one family would be punished for something the children of another family would be allowed to get away with! Meals together round the great oak table in the dining room could be a major trial, and I well remember Colin's thunderous face at the head of the table on several occasions when things got a bit out of hand with the children.

But this time was incredibly rich in terms of teaching. Colin was reading Watchman Nee's *The Spiritual Man*, popularly referred to as 'The Red Book' in the community, and at every morning prayer time over a long period, when all the community was gathered, he would expound from this book and the Scriptures. The teaching was a complete revelation to me. I was born again and baptised in the Holy Spirit well before joining the Bethany Fellowship, but as Colin's teaching impinged on my heart I began to doubt my spiritual status altogether. The revelation was the division between soul and spirit, two entities which I had previously assumed

71

to be one and the same thing. Watchman Nee showed so clearly that they were diametrically opposed (see Hebrews 4:12 and Galatians 5:16–18), and it seemed to me that my whole life was lived at soul (or sinful nature) level, that is at the level of the mind, will and emotions, and I had not allowed the Holy Spirit to rule my life as I thought.

Colin's teaching, as always, was clear, reasoned and backed by Scripture and had a life-changing effect on me. I seemed to be in tears most of the time for the first three months of our stay at The Hyde. There were plenty of opportunities given for repentance, and Colin would see each of us individually from time to time to pray with and for us. It was almost like a confessional and it was pretty serious stuff; one did not fool around with Colin especially when those steely blue eyes seemed to bore right into one's heart. He would hear what one had to say, prompt with accurate questioning and almost always receive an encouraging scripture or vision for the person as they prayed together at the end of the session.

What of Colin's own walk with the Lord?

This remained private for the most part. He was indeed a very private person, unapproachable in normal social terms and devoid of small talk, and this combined with the spiritual power that operated through him meant that we respected and, yes, feared him. It was not possible to get to know Colin as a person or have an ordinary social relationship with him, but we all knew we were benefitting hugely through the ministry of this prophet who headed up the community and who envisioned all of us with faith for revival in Britain and mighty things to come through the Fellowship. I am greatly indebted to Colin for all that I have learnt through his teaching both personally and in terms of ministry. Much of the time at The Hyde was hard, but there was also great joy and I would not have missed it for anything. The close relationships built with other members of the community have endured. We went through so many deep experiences together.

The Old Testament prophets and the disciples in the New

Testament could not have been easy people to live with: Colin, a present-day prophet, was not an easy person to live with. Most, if not all of us, in Bethany suffered hurt of one kind or another through Colin's inability to relate on a personal level to people, and this in itself was a growth point if one knew how to overcome it (Romans 5:3–4). This difficulty showed itself through leadership decisions as well, quite often taken without due regard to other leaders and members of the Fellowship who would be affected, but with more of an eye towards 'higher' kingdom issues.

At various times there has been an exodus of people from the Fellowship, none more so than when Colin moved his centre of operations to Roffey Place and The Hyde was vacated. A plethora of new ministries has been created by ex-Bethany members who have been trained in a tough school, and each one owes something to a man of unwavering faith and ambition for God's kingdom.

Charles and Joyce Sibthorpe

On September 1st, 1979, Charles and Joyce Sibthorpe and their five children moved into a cottage in the grounds. They were to work with Colin until August 31st, 1987. Charles was born and brought up in Cornwall, where he had also spent his entire working life. Charles and Joyce first met Colin in November 1977 when he visited Cornwall to teach on renewal. Colin recalls a dramatic event that weekend:

We were sitting having a leisurely cup of coffee when we heard screams. One of the boys came rushing into the kitchen: 'Dad, there's been an accident.' Charles didn't wait to hear any more. He ran out of the house and across the yard, closely followed by Joyce.

Caroline and I were staying with Charles and Joyce and their family, while I was ministering for a few days in Cornwall. On the previous evening I had been speaking about the prayer promises of Jesus and what it means to pray with faith, knowing that God is going to answer you.

We were already praying when Charles carried ten-year-old Joanna into the room. In the garage the children had been melting down lead to pour into moulds, to make gifts for Christmas. One of them dropped a cold piece of metal into the container causing some of the molten mixture to fly into Joanna's face.

Some of the liquid lead had gone into both eyes. Can you imagine the effect of molten lead on eyes?

It took her mother nearly forty minutes to remove all the pieces of metal. During that time we all prayed, silently and aloud, with Joanna and for her. But all the time we thanked the Lord that there would be no damage to the eyes, and praised Him for His healing.[2]

Joanna slept, and at 5 p.m. was back downstairs having tea, her eyes not even bloodshot. Subsequently it was confirmed medically that no damage to her eyes had been caused at all.

Eighteen months later, in April 1979, Colin made a return visit to Cornwall. At that time Charles was organising 'Mission Cornwall', but felt that the enterprise lacked cohesion and clear-cut objectives. Colin invited Charles and Joyce to visit The Hyde to pray and think about their future. This they did in June 1979 when God spoke clearly to them about revival and, more pertinently, about joining Colin's ministry team. By September 1979 the Sibthorpes were settled at The Hyde, by which time the community had jumped to twenty-nine people: fifteen adults and fourteen children.

What were Charles's impressions after working with Colin for fully eight years? This is what he told me:

I enjoyed a good working relationship with Colin. I was part of the leadership team at The Hyde (with David Brown) and co-ordinated Colin's travelling programme, previously the province of George Hoerder. I travelled a lot with him and

74

throughout our time together although we disagreed, there was never any sense of animosity between us.

Colin's ministry and teaching affected my life in a number of key ways. Before going to The Hyde both my wife and I had experienced the baptism of the Holy Spirit, so we had a framework of faith as a starting-point, but Colin helped shape that framework for us personally and theologically. At an inspirational level, he brought truth directly into our lives, as we observed his constant desire to enact the Word of God in our daily behaviour. He also had enormous spiritual integrity.

Colin was definitely a man of prophetic vision, he heard God's voice over such things as the Leaders' Weeks and the purchase of Roffey Place.

A man of vision then, but he didn't always know *how* to work out his vision; and he failed to appoint men at the second level of leadership who had sufficient quality to put into practice that vision. He failed to have a creative and dynamic second lieutenant, if you like, who would challenge his perceptions as well as put his ideas into an effective form.

Strategic teaching

Throughout 1979 and 1980 Colin's teaching at The Hyde was dominated by three themes in particular, all of which are seminal for an understanding of his whole ministry.

The first theme is that of kingdom authority. This emphasis grew partly out of what Colin observed as he travelled the world. He was aware of negative responses, faithless statements and generally unbelieving attitudes in the lives of so many people. They frequently shared with Colin their feelings of being absolutely defeated in their everyday lives, thus exhibiting a paradox. As he says, 'If we are to live "in Christ Jesus" we obviously cannot live in pessimism, failure and defeat.' Colin saw the whole matter in terms of realising the authority that

Christians possess, the secret of which is complete submission to Jesus's authority and lordship in our daily experience:

> The more we are submitted to Him, the more of His authority is seen in us. People had often remarked to me on the note of authority in my preaching. That caused neither pride nor complacency, for I constantly recognised the need for more of the authority of Jesus in my ministry. Faith and the use of authority go together in the gospels and are seen supremely in the ministry of Jesus. His authority mastered every situation. I was only too aware of the many occasions when I had insufficient of the Lord's authority to see His victory in those particular circumstances. That caused me to seek the Lord still further, not so much for more of His power, but to be submitted completely to Him. I was not content with what I saw happening, but more concerned about what I didn't see taking place.[3]

He saw 'new life' in Jesus, too, as an authority and a power to act today in the name of Jesus, and in *Faith for the Future* he strikes this very definite note:

> We inherit those same commands that Jesus gave to His disciples. He makes available the same power and authority to His Church today as He did to His Church then. So much hinges on knowing that this is yours as a child of the Kingdom.
>
> It must be possible to speak to the mountains of need in other people's lives and command them to move in the name of Jesus. Obviously this has to be done under the direction and anointing of the Holy Spirit, for Jesus would not have acted in any other way.[4]

The second theme Colin emphasised was *kingdom faith*. This, he taught, begins with a personal acceptance of the victory of the cross over sin and death. It expresses itself in a hunger for the Word of God and in a desire to take the gospel beyond the immediate confines of the church to the nation at large. Here we are touching the nerve centre of his ministry: his conviction that God wants a powerful and effective church so operating in faith that it ushers in revival; a revival that affects the economic, political, social and spiritual life of the country. Not merely pockets of revival, largely restricted to certain churches, but a cataclysm, a revolution that transforms the life of Britain in its entirety. It remains his vision to this day.

A third major theme in Colin's teaching was what it means to be 'in Christ Jesus'. This important New Testament teaching[5] is also the title of one of Colin's books, in which he explores three great revelations of the New Testament: God's action in history in Jesus; the foundational truths regarding a Christian's new life in Jesus; and the ways in which Christians are meant to live in Him. The central argument is spelled out exhaustively under different headings; one quotation must suffice:

> In Him I have died and can count myself dead to sin. Of myself I am still prone to sin. In Him my old nature has no power, sin is not my master and cannot control me. But if I set my mind on the things of the flesh, on pleasing myself, on my own weakness and failure, I shall fear, doubt, sin – and deny my inheritance in Christ every time I do so.

Marketing the vision

In the early and formative days of the Bethany Fellowship, Colin's teaching on these aspects of New Testament truth – his vision, if you like – was developed and applied to the Fellowship at The Hyde by David Brown, and to the wider community beyond West Sussex by Charles Sibthorpe. Kingdom Faith missions were organised throughout the length and breadth of Britain, and team members were confronted by the plea for basic Christian biblical teaching. The response to this sort of request was the Kingdom Faith Teaching Course which led people from the point of conversion through the various stages to growth and maturity. The format for this course was Charles Sibthorpe's idea:

> Each month a cassette would be made available, containing four twenty-minute talks, one for each week. These could be used privately but were intended primarily for use in small groups. Together with the cassette tape, work sheets would be made available. These would refer people to the relevant Scriptures, ask questions to draw out the substance of the teaching, and suggest ways in which the Word could be expressed in the daily lives of the listeners.

A limited number of advertisements were placed in the Christian press in the summer of 1980 with a view to beginning the course in September. The response was staggering: six hundred groups enrolled immediately, indicating the extent of the need for such teaching and the hunger in people's lives.

Charles also had a vision for Leaders' Weeks at The Hyde, when leaders of all denominations could come for spiritual refreshment. These weeks, just like the teaching course, became an instant success.

Another important development concerned the 'Living in Revival' weeks, also based at The Hyde. While not directly involved in the organisation and running of these ventures, Colin often spoke at some of the key sessions, thus setting the tone for much of what went on. Together with the Bethany Fellowship members, he helped create an atmosphere of faith, expectancy and healing in which people who were damaged by life or churches, or both, could find a new place of peace and contentment 'in Christ Jesus'. Hundreds of testimonies could be quoted to attest to this fact, but one is sufficient to illustrate the nature and completeness of the work that proved so beneficial to so many people.

The person whose testimony I am quoting below (we shall call

her 'Janet') had previously suffered an acute depressive illness
and had only very reluctantly agreed to attend the 'Living in
Revival' course which ran from Monday afternoon to Thursday
lunchtime. The time scale is mentioned if only to indicate the
extent of healing that took place. This is Janet's testimony:

In April 1984 I went to the Bethany Fellowship on a Living
in Revival week. My husband had been on a similar course
in January of that year and had come back very different,
so it was with mixed feelings that I settled in at The Hyde.

The praise and worship was very spontaneous and free, and
I was embarrassed by the freedom with which most people
expressed their feelings. But, as I began to relax and look
around me I noticed that people's expressions were really
beautiful; they were obviously lost in wonder, love and praise
for their heavenly Father. Suddenly in my heart I began to
feel envious of their deep love for the Lord and their trust
in a way that I just didn't feel at all. I knew in my head that
I loved God and that I had accepted Christ as my saviour,
but I didn't feel he loved me because of everything that had
happened to me after the birth of one of my daughters and
my post-natal depression.

On the Tuesday Charles Sibthorpe spoke on the cross. He
said that we had to come afresh to the cross for cleansing
and forget our pride, and he also mentioned the victory
Christ had won for us on the cross. My heart was deeply
touched and I found tears pouring down my face as I faced
again what Jesus had done for *me*. I ran out of the room
and up to my bedroom where I lay on the floor and through
my sobs began to see myself as God saw me: full of anger,
bitterness because of my illness and all the traumatic events
that accompanied it: the shock treatment, loss of memory,
the despair, the isolation, the attempted suicide, and all the
degrading and humiliating happenings that occur with this
type of illness that can emotionally scar a person for life.

I realised, as I lay on the floor, that all my sufferings were
nothing compared to what Christ had been through for me.
There and then I came once again to the foot of the cross
and asked for forgiveness – for my anger, bitterness and

resentment towards God, my unfeeling attitude towards others suffering like me, towards my husband, my mother and my sister: 'Why can't she understand what it is like to have a child who doesn't sleep?' At this stage I felt empty, but I did begin to enjoy the praise and worship, the prayer times, and I began to feel the presence of God in the various meetings.

Later in the week I went for a walk on my own in the grounds of The Hyde, found a bench and began to pray. The Lord showed me other areas of my life that had grieved Him and I again repented. I walked on up a hill and looked up wondering which way to go as the grounds were sparsely wooded, while to the left of me I saw a densely wooded area that looked dark, so I didn't want to go that way. On the right was a beautiful field, fresh and bright and green, and I had an overwhelming desire to go and run and dance in it. I thought, 'This place is really getting to me, I must be mad,' but I did that and then jumped hastily back over the fence.

That same evening Charles spoke, and as he did so I listened with a sense of anticipation that something was going to happen. I also felt nervous as I didn't want to cry again. He spoke about his own personal experience, the lack of power in his life, his fears and lack of faith until he asked the Lord to fill him with His Holy Spirit, and I knew that was what I needed to do. At the close of the meeting I went forward with a throbbing heart, various people laid their hands on me, and Charles prayed a beautiful prayer about God's Holy Spirit being a perfect gentleman, only going where he is asked, and that He was going to come into my life and heal me of all the past hurts.

Oh, the love and peace and joy I felt: it was almost unbelievable. I felt I was free and running in that beautiful field I had seen that afternoon, I just couldn't stop praising the Lord, I just wanted to tell Him all the time how much I loved Him and I knew and *felt* His love for me, His pleasure and love towards *me* as a person. My week at The Hyde was truly a turning point in my life.

It is interesting to compare what happened to Janet's husband when he attended a Living in Revival course. Born and brought up in a Brethren family, he had always understood that the baptism in the Holy Spirit occurs to everyone at the point of conversion. He went rather unwillingly to the course. This is what occurred:

> The first thing that struck me was the sheer uninhibited joy of the people there. They all seemed to be alive in a powerful but perfectly sincere way. I didn't much like the choruses which seemed banal and full of the most dreadful cliches; however I had to admit that the room was filled with a power I had not previously experienced.
>
> On the Tuesday morning Colin Urquhart spoke about the angel's words to Mary, 'Fear not' (Luke 2:10) and then applied those words in a number of different ways. He also spoke about several different Brethren churches' reactions to healing, the gifts of the Spirit and, oh dear, the baptism in the Spirit. What possible interest could there be for me in all of this? I knew the answers, the biblical teaching, etc., and was not at all impressed. Colin was obviously sincere in his beliefs but it all appeared rather extreme to me.
>
> That day, too, Charles took us through some teaching by Charles Finney on revival, including a list of, I think, almost thirty things people needed to repent of before God would bless them with personal revival. I perused the list rather gloomily, felt most of them applied to me, the only one I definitely wasn't guilty of was adultery! I did repent of all those I was guilty of and, strangely, felt better in my spirit.
>
> I was still not convinced about the baptism in the Spirit and rehearsed my arguments against this experience to one of the helpers (Marion Hawkins) who quietly and wisely said: 'Let Jesus minister to you.' And that night, in prayer with a number of other people, I did just that and I entered into this experience, and spoke in tongues too. That Living in Revival course changed my whole life.

What is interesting about both testimonies is that there was obviously a sense of corporate anointing on The Hyde and the helpers there. There was also a clear feeling of freedom and an atmosphere of worship. All these factors contributed to the changes in Janet's perceptions and feelings. Charles's honesty and openness in describing his own experience to her was crucial, as was the straightforward and practical exposition of the Word of God. On a platform of praise and worship, Janet was brought into the life-transforming experience of the baptism in the Spirit (as was her husband), and all in a natural and unforced way. No pressure or hype was necessary; instead, in both cases God did His work with someone willing – and needing – to be changed in a radical fashion. Similar testimonies were repeated innumerable times on other Living in Revival weeks at The Hyde, which became an integral and vital part of the Bethany Fellowship's outreach and influence that extended throughout the country.

Building up the work

By the end of 1980 Colin, his family and members of the Fellowship were firmly – and busily – established at The Hyde. He continued to travel the length and breadth of Britain with messages of holiness, faith and revival: kingdom life, in other words. His preaching, in general, found a ready acceptance, especially with men and women who were prepared to open and expose their lives to the demands of his teaching, which was always decidedly Christ-centred and challenging.

Churches eager to discover more about the life of the Spirit welcomed him warmly, and frequently weekend conferences developed into mini revivals ('times of refreshing'), reminiscent of Pentecost itself. These occasions naturally encouraged Colin and his team a great deal. They did not surprise Colin because he had absolute faith in God to reveal Himself in power and in signs and wonders whenever the Word of God was preached in power.

By now, too, leadership structures at The Hyde were clearly established, with Colin, Charles Sibthorpe and David Brown recognised as elders of the Bethany Fellowship. The latter two took responsibility for the day-to-day running when Colin travelled abroad. This structure, with its intentional plurality of leadership and diversity of gifts and rôles, is essentially different from the vast majority of Anglican churches where there is one clearly-defined leader who undertakes the bulk of the work. While Colin may have been accepted as 'first among equals', the structure had a flexibility that enabled Charles and David to develop their own areas of ministry. It also included the vitally important feature of mutual accountability.

Much had been achieved during the period 1978–80 but, as always, Colin constantly looked to the future, and he sensed that 1981 would be 'different'. So it was to prove, though not just in positive ways.

8

LOCALISED REVIVAL

1981 was the year in which radical decisions were made which affected the outreach of the Fellowship. One such decision concerned the question of Kingdom Faith Ministries. It was decided that instead of hopping around the country – often on extremely tight schedules – from one meeting to another, the team should concentrate on a series of short five-day missions with a primary evangelistic thrust. This would have the advantage of allowing team members to go flat out, in a given location, for a relatively short period of time, after which they could return to home base to recover, pray and analyse the event that had just taken place.

On these missions, Colin and his team found many churches existing on a low level of faith, with expectancy for the future the last thing on the agenda. In such churches, they were able to bring a new and dynamic impetus to church life. Colin was constantly amazed at the positive ways people responded to an essentially simple and direct method of operation. At these meetings there were no frills or gimmicks, but simply the preaching of the Word of God on a platform of worship. There was most definitely expectancy, the belief and faith that God would manifest himself where there was unity of heart, spirit and purpose amongst the team. Indeed, as Psalm 133 makes clear, where such unity exists, God is commanded to bless, which is what happened regularly and wonderfully. There was no intention to make the occasions 'healing' meetings as such, but that's what occurred very often. Naturally some churches found supernatural healings disconcerting, but Colin and his team were convinced that this was the right approach to adopt.

Revival

Even more radical and fundamental for the life of the Bethany Fellowship was the localised revival that took place in May 1981. Since Easter the community at The Hyde, aided by Charles Finney's classic exposition on revival, *Finney on Revival*, had been preoccupied with the convicting power and cleansing of the Holy Spirit that has often been the prelude to revival in many different countries.

Colin guided the team into a consideration of those factors which had been instructive in his own life and experience. He also dealt with those things which hinder revival on a personal and individual level:

> A lack of gratitude and love towards God; neglect of the Bible, prayer, family duties, watchfulness over oneself and one's brethren; neglect of self-denial and the means of grace. God's purposes are further hindered by unbelief, worldly-mindedness, pride, envy, slander, censoriousness, levity, lying, cheating, hypocrisy, robbing God, bad temper and hindering others from being useful.[1]

He emphasised the need for revival in the *minds* of members of the community:

> They were a battlefield; we had thoughts we did not want and that were dishonouring to the Lord; unholy thoughts, impure thoughts, proud thoughts, selfish thoughts, wandering thoughts when praying, and so on. The mind is the first line of attack for the enemy. If he can disrupt our thinking, he will succeed in robbing us of peace and

will sow confusion and anxiety instead. And our thinking determines our actions; wrong thinking will produce wrong actions.[2]

Many members of the community did indeed search their hearts and did repent in a new and fresh way, thus releasing again the Holy Spirit into their lives, purging away the dross and replacing it with the life of the Spirit.

Colin also realised that there was yet a further dimension: holiness. He understood, and taught, that without a meeting with God in all His pristine holiness, all the previous repentance would remain unfruitful in terms of true personal and corporate revival. His teaching bore a rich harvest of fruit. This is his account of what happened next:

> It was Friday, May 1st, 1981. The members of the mission team were praying together. Ahead lay the spring holiday weekend, a time when we could be with our families before the busy summer of travelling for the missions. On the following Tuesday we would be off on a whirlwind tour of meetings to prepare for these missions.
>
> Suddenly there came the realisation that whatever this revival was that needed to happen to us, it hadn't happened. We still did not have the Lord's faith for these missions.
>
> I was crying out in my heart to God. 'What do we have to do, Lord?' I felt a great agony in my soul. He answered my prayer: 'Abandon all your plans for the weekend and seek me.' I shared that with the others and the reaction of some was plain. For us, a long weekend with our families was a luxury. But the Lord made it clear that if we were not prepared to face the cost of such a sacrifice we could forget the rest. What had Charles Finney said about the cost of revival?
>
> The news soon spread throughout the community. Saturday would be a day of prayer and all the adults would meet together at seven p.m.
>
> On that Saturday I sensed a longing in some to meet with

the Lord. That was certainly the desire in my heart. In others there was reticence, a fear perhaps. As the day progressed people were moved by the Spirit to confess their negative responses and seek the Lord's forgiveness.

Saturday, May 2nd, seven p.m. The community meets together, packed into the library at The Hyde. The praise and singing begins. Silence falls upon the gathering. A few confess their negative reactions at having to spend the holiday seeking the Lord; others express their longing to meet with Him.

A simple prayer is forming in my heart: 'Lord, please come and meet with us in your holiness.' Inwardly I begin to pray those words over and over again, begging the Lord to respond to them. I speak the same prayer out loud and it is echoed by several others. The Holy Spirit has created the same desire in their hearts.

There is a word of prophecy. God speaks to the hearts of His children and suddenly it seems that Jesus walks into the room, the Holy Jesus. Immediately people start falling to their knees. Next they are lying prostrate, on their faces before the Lord. One person after another is crying out to the Lord for His mercy. Open confession of sin is happening, one person after another. The secrets of hearts are being revealed. The presence of others doesn't matter; nothing can remain hidden in the Holy Presence of Jesus. There is only longing to be right with the risen Saviour.

There are many tears, much beseeching of the Lord in tongues, many praying aloud at once. An hour, two hours and still people are prostrate before the Lord. Many have come to a place of peace; more than that, they are clean. 'Create in me a clean heart, O God, and renew a right spirit within me,' King David had prayed.

The Lord had come among us and revealed His holiness. In those brief hours the Lord had shown more to us about our hearts than all our weeks of searching had revealed.[3]

This sense of the presence of the holiness of God continued through Sunday and Monday. Then came Monday evening:

Above left: Colin during his school days at St. Paul's.

Above right: Colin and Caroline's favourite wedding photograph.

Right: Colin during his time at St Hugh's.

Left: Caroline and first born, Claire, in 1966.

Below: Clive, Andrea and Claire.

Bottom: An artist's impression of St Hugh's in Lewsey, Luton.

Above: The worship at St Hugh's.

Below: The family during the time at St Hugh's.

Below right: Christmas party event.

The Hyde at Handcross, a beautiful house sited in 28 glorious acres.

The house at Bolney where Colin, Caroline and family, with a household of about 12 others, spent six and a half years.

Above left: Clive, when 16 years, who became a drummer with Heartbeat and is now Youth Pastor of Kingdom Faith Church.

Above right: Andrea.

Below: Colin and Caroline with Archbishop Benson Idahosa and his wife, Margaret when they visited the Hyde.

Above left: Singapore Cathedral service at which Colin preached.

Above right: A favourite photograph of Caroline.

Below: Dancing before God at the altar with the former Archbishop of Capetown, the Rt. Revd. Bill Burnett, together with 30 other bishops.

Above: The same occasion as the previous picture.

Right: Colin and Caroline cutting their Silver Wedding cake at Roffey Place surrounded by members of the team.

Roffey Place, the present base for Kingdom Faith Ministries.

Urquhart Castle on the shores of Lockness, a photograph taken by Colin but not quite the family seat.

As on the previous two evenings, there was open repentance, leading to a great sense of the Lord's peace and worship before His throne. But then the unexpected happened. The room was not only filled with the holiness of God, but with His glory!

It has been difficult enough to explain events so far; now no words can be found to describe what followed. People were no longer on their faces; everyone was standing, arms extended to heaven, exalting God with loud voices, shouting praises to Him. And He was there in majesty, in glory, in honour.[3]

The intensity and awesomeness of the experience was so overwhelming that Colin felt he would never be the same again. How had this revival come about?

Reasons for revival

In the first place, the Bethany Fellowship had gone through a period of genuine and deeply-rooted repentance which led to frank confession of sin, a putting right of wrong relationships, and an honest dealing with wrong and unhelpful habits.

In the second place, Colin had taught the community systematically and carefully over an extended period of time, outlining not only the need for, but also the prerequisite, of revival. The people were informed about the nature of revival and the theology of revival, too. Doctrine was stressed as the indispensable guide to behaviour. In this sense Colin's teaching was practical and realistic.

In the third place, there was a collective seeking for and demonstration of the holiness of God.

Charles Sibthorpe, one of the participants that May 1981 weekend, has reflected on these events and, in his book *A Man Under Authority*, discusses the effects of revival. In his view, revival releases God's light into a person's life. The example he cites is powerful because it is personal:

In the middle of all that God was doing during the summer of 1981, I suddenly discovered that one of the girls in the team was having an effect on me that was both disturbing and difficult to understand. It did not seem to have arisen out of my action or hers. Nothing overt was happening between us. My marriage was under no strain and my love for Joyce was continuing to grow and become stronger rather than weaker. No, this seemed to be an attack from the enemy who was trying to bring darkness into my life and to promote sin.

I was puzzling over this, having prayed about it, when it occurred to me that I should have a chat with David Brown, one of my fellow elders. I went to see him in his study one morning and told him the situation, looking for his help. He simply said: 'Now you have walked in the light with me about this you don't need to worry any more. The enemy's power is broken.' He was right. I walked out of that room a free man. I saw a new depth of meaning in Romans 10:10 – 'For it is with your heart that you believe and are justified, and it is with your mouth that you confess and are saved.' Walking in the light produces victory over temptation and sin; however, just a word of warning – open confession that is too detailed and intimate can do more harm than good. For example, to confess lustful thoughts will cause no problem if described simply by those two words, but any more detail would be harmful to the hearers and would not release any more healing into the life of the person making the confession.[4]

Revival also, he comments, produces power prayer:

On the Tuesday that followed the weekend of meeting with God, we were up early and set out for Grimsby where we were to hold a pre-mission rally. Even as we drove up the motorway we realized that something was different. Normally we would chat, listen to some praise cassettes or perhaps some teaching. This time, all we wanted to do was to pray and worship the Lord.

When we arrived at the Ice House and set up all the equipment, we were planning our time so as to leave the normal half hour of prayer before the start of the meeting. We now found this to be totally inadequate and had to reschedule our daily timetable so as to have two hours of prayer before each meeting.

These times were not simply for praying about the meeting, but revival prayer in the presence of God when he could liberate his power in and through us. That which had characterized the revival weekend continued. Open confession of sin came naturally and quickly. There was a tremendous sense of God's peace and we were constantly aware of his holy presence among us. There was a new release of faith for the ministry and a fresh concern for the lost.[5]

Charles Sibthorpe also found that revival liberates love and unity. This liberation was extremely important for those who worked closely together, both at The Hyde and in other parts of the country. Nothing so effectively hinders the work of God as disunity, while the outflow of love and unity can have only one effect: the more effective working of God's life amongst Christians and, in the long run, amongst those who are not Christians.

Revival also results in a hunger for God, of the sort found in Psalm 42: yearning, panting for God, not the tepid piety that so often masquerades for the life of the Spirit in our country today. This hunger, in turn, leads to further revival, further power, further glory.

During this period, there was a cohesion present in The Hyde, a cutting edge and a unity about the revival which was a watershed in the lives of a number of people, a significant turning-point in their relationship with God and with each other. Not surprisingly, they did not want that experience, or related set of circumstances, to come to an end. They see it as a critical stage in their spiritual development when certain fundamental lessons were learned which continue to have validity today. Amongst these is the realisation that revival *must* begin with the people of God, men and women desirous to see God at work in life-changing ways. The unsaved can scarcely be 'revived' unless God's people are: that is the very basis of revival. Another is the awareness that revival is God's sovereign work, which cannot be manipulated, artificially produced, cunningly imitated, or brought into being at the drop of a hat: revival has to be prepared for in a serious and biblical way. A third lesson is that seminal to all revivals is an understanding of God's essential holiness and splendour. Equally important is the desire to go on being renewed and revived on a daily and continuous basis.

Why not revival in Britain?

Many people at The Hyde at this time saw the events as so comprehensive and thorough-going that they wondered if this localised revival would be a springboard for something much greater and more extensive: national revival, that majestic sweep of God's sovereign power and holiness that transforms a country in all aspects of its life, not just the churches. Why not, the question was asked, revival in Britain instead of merely a pocket of revival in West Sussex?

Charles Sibthorpe is of the opinion that three related factors explain the fact that the localised revival at The Hyde did not break out on a wider stage. The first factor, as he sees it, was an internal debate amongst the trustees of the Bethany Fellowship. One trustee in particular feared that Colin was about to renounce the Church of England and launch his own brand of house church. As a consequence, this person resigned as a trustee of the fellowship and opposed Colin both nationally and internationally. This rebuke inevitably caused Colin great damage in the short term and his leadership undoubtedly struggled.

The second factor, in Charles's view, was Colin's failure to give decisive leadership. Strong creative leadership was required to spearhead the vision for revival in Britain, but after Colin spent a month moving house, from The Hyde to Bolney, in April 1982, a vacuum existed, with an overall lack of clarity and sense of purpose. The move was undertaken in order to release accommodation for other members of the growing Fellowship. Perfectly reasonable in itself, it nevertheless, in Charles's opinion, had a detrimental effect in terms of the revival spreading outside the confines of the Fellowship's base in Sussex.

The third factor, according to Charles, was the changing nature of the leadership at the fellowship. By the summer of 1982, five men were looked upon as 'the leaders': Colin himself, David Brown, Bob Gordon, Michael Barling and Charles Sibthorpe. Colin was commonly accepted as the final authority in matters of fellowship organisation and practice, while the others were carving out their own particular niche and sphere of operation. David Brown, for example, felt increasingly drawn towards work amongst drug addicts, alcoholics and down-and-outs, an interest and a drive that led eventually to the purchase of Abbot's Leigh and the work at 'The City' in Brighton. Charles was constrained to develop the work of revival amongst church leaders as well as the 'Living in Revival' weeks. Michael Barling, too, was trying to find his place in the Fellowship and did not feel equipped to give administrative form and shape to Colin's vision for national revival. These facts, Charles believes, all conspired together to blunt the edge of a possible spread of revival in terms of the nation. A sense of disappointment was inevitable, and Colin seemed unable to assemble – or did not have available to him – an additional stratum of leadership with sufficient quality to put the vision into action. Soon, too, another faith project began to attract Colin and his fellow leaders: Roffey Place, to which story we shall turn in the next chapter.

What, then, did Colin make of it all?

God's sovereign timing

Colin does not accept Charles's argued viewpoint. He offers the inescapably correct biblical dictum that as revival is a sovereign act of God, nothing can prevent such an out-pouring taking place were it meant to happen. He also points to the fact that, in a very *limited* sense, the localised revival did affect the nation. This happened with the series of major crusades conducted by the fellowship throughout Britain. On these occasions a wider audience began to appreciate what the revival dynamic is.

Most important of all, however, in Colin's view is the prophetic word received at the beginning of the revival at The Hyde. God spoke directly, saying: 'This is only a foretaste of the revival that is coming to the nation in a few years, and this foretaste will last only for a few months.' Hence, for Colin, God had made it clear from the start that the foretaste they were experiencing was only going to last for a short period of time. Nothing he could have done, therefore, would have turned it into a national revival. Colin also understood from the prophetic word that the coming revival would impact the *whole* nation, not just parts of it. He has clung tenaciously to this prophecy ever since, concluding that back in 1982 the time was not right for the sort of explosion of God's life that Charles thought possible.

These views are different sides of a coin, and signal the possibility of a lost opportunity at that time. What is indisputable is that the nation of Britain, in all its moral, social and spiritual need, still awaits God's divine touch in a way that large-scale evangelism scarcely touches. Meanwhile, Colin retains his vision that revival is, indeed, coming to this country. He is also of the opinion that Roffey Place has a strategic rôle to play in any future out-pouring of God's power. The story of the acquisition of Roffey Place is truly exciting and encouraging; it is the story of faith rewarded.

9

ROFFEY PLACE CHRISTIAN
TRAINING CENTRE

It would be difficult to imagine two more contrasting figures than Colin Urquhart and Bob Gordon. Colin is quiet to the point of being taciturn, Bob is a rumbustious extrovert. Colin seldom talks about himself, Bob tends to wear his heart on his sleeve. Colin almost never talks about his family. Bob frequently refers to his father and his godly influence upon him. Colin is a reflective visionary, Bob makes visions happen in a practical and direct way. Colin is more a man of prayer, while Bob is pre-eminently a man of action, vigorous and demanding. Colin is patient and persevering, Bob gets easily bored. Colin is essentially an exhorter, Bob is a teacher *par excellence*, as those who heard his sermons on James at the Faith '84 convention would readily agree. Colin's background, apart from his years at King's College, London, was neither academic nor evangelical, while Bob's was both. Yet, they worked together to great effect from the early part of 1982 until July 1989.

A fruitful partnership

The partnership of Colin and Bob came about in a slightly roundabout way. Bob left his United Reformed church in Durham (where he was also a university chaplain) at the end of 1978 and came to London with the hope of working with the Fountain Trust, which was led by the Reverend Tom Smail at that time. For one year he worked alongside them, but not as part of the staff, until it became clear that the Fountain Trust was going to close down. He was then asked to become a Lecturer in Old Testament Studies at London Bible College where he stayed until 1982. Although he enjoyed the experience at L.B.C. very much, he felt increasingly that academic life was not the reason he had left his church in Durham. During these years he met with a group of influential charismatic leaders at The Hyde.

At the beginning of 1982 Bob was increasingly exercised in his spirit about the direction of his future ministry, but he felt no draw at all to the Bethany Fellowship or to West Sussex. One day, however, while he was attending one of the meetings at the Hyde, the Spirit of God spoke clearly to him that this was where he was meant to be. Bob explains: 'At that time I did not feel that it meant I should be part of the Bethany Fellowship or Colin's team but that I should live in proximity and fellowship for mutual benefit.'

This happened very quickly and 'the Lord opened the way through the provision to buy a house, and Hilda and I and two singles came to live at Tilgate Forest Lodge only a mile or so away from The Hyde'.

Bob very quickly entered into a good personal relationship with Colin and the other elders and within a short time found himself deeply involved in the work and eldership of the ministry. At that period Colin was out of the country ministering quite a lot and Bob found himself drawn into the day-to-day running of certain aspects of the work, alongside Charles Sibthorpe and others. Colin and Bob developed a respect for each other and a trust which manifested itself in the way they worked together in the development of major parts of the ministry, for example, the start of the Faith Camps (held for one week each year at the beginning of August), which combine worship sessions with teaching on key aspects of Christianity, for all ages, from children upwards. These camps continue to this day.

Colin's influence

Colin's teaching and example did not deepen Bob's biblical understanding in one sense because, as he says, 'the background and experience I came from was deeply biblical and, indeed, sometimes I found myself dissatisfied with the teaching that was given'. He did, though, as he readily admits, come to see the power of the Word of God in a more radical way, which he believes Colin has always tried to make the foundation of his ministry.

Bob identifies three major areas where he learned fundamental lessons from Colin personally:

> The first was confidence in ministry. Through my relationship with and working with Colin I found my spirit quickened as far as the application of the Word was concerned. Colin always aims to drive the Word into action and response, and this has had a profound effect within my own ministry. The second was strength of faith. Whether I always agreed with his sermons or not I learned to admire his perseverance of spirit and, at times, found this a great challenge to my own attitudes or actions.

The third area in which Colin influenced Bob was in determination of character: 'I don't know how Colin would see himself, but he presents a strong sense of purpose. Once he has got hold of something, he is not easily shaken if he feels it is right. This determination comes from depths in his nature and is, I believe, one of the secrets of his leadership of other people.'

Intriguingly, Bob now feels that, 'the whole experience of working with and listening to Colin has done something for my biblical understanding. It has provided a clear reference point for what I believe and, in many ways, for how I act.' There were lessons for Bob, too, in the area of life-style:

> It taught me a great deal on the positive side about attitudes to possessions and sharing. It helped me to see what was of practical and economic necessity as opposed to theological necessity. I thought then and still do so that some things were presented as divine revelation when in fact they were expedient to the situation. This does not make them wrong or right, it simply means that there are more ways to skin a cat than one.

Bob stresses key areas in which Colin had a beneficial influence upon him, but also points to issues which divided them. He comments, 'Once Colin had got an idea he was not easily put off. He had a deep passion to see God working in revival power today. He has great strength of character and perseverance to see things through.' Bob adds that 'Colin's strength can also be his weakness: what is a great blessing in certain areas of ministry can become an oppressive influence to others.'

The picture also emerges, from what Bob says, of someone who leads 'from the top' through inspiration, rather than 'on the ground' through personal relationships. This means as in many things that it is difficult for people to question his leadership because it might be seen as spiritual rebellion rather than honest questioning. Undoubtedly this is connected with Colin's view of revelation and authority. For the major part of Bob's time with Colin he saw himself as 'a go-between' (his description) in this kind of situation, and he felt that the incipient tension of their situation was its very strength. The particular distinctives in their public ministries was what gave the earlier Faith Camps their colour and balance: many people saw this as fruitful and creative.

The high-point of their partnership was undoubtedly the

purchase and foundation of Roffey Place Christian Training Centre.

An adventure of faith

The prime movers in the purchase of Roffey Place (purpose-built for use as a college) were Colin and Bob: it represented a shared vision on their part. The building had been, for five years, the national headquarters of the Royal Society for the Prevention of Cruelty to Animals. It had been extensively refurbished, but by 1983 it was no longer considered appropriate for the ongoing and developing work of the Society, who put it up for sale at a price of £600,000. Its structure, facilities and general equipment were attractive by any standards.

Colin and Bob, however, looked beyond the immediate and obvious appeal of the building to the fulfilment of a vision that both men had nurtured, quite independently of each other, for a number of years. Bob outlines that vision in his book, *Out of the Melting Pot*:

> I had felt for a long time the need to be able to disciple men and women into the deeper ways of God through the work of the Holy Spirit – especially men and women who themselves were involved in ministry and leadership, so that they could come to understand the principles of ministering in the power of the Holy Spirit today.[1]

To minister 'in the power of the Holy Spirit' requires faith, an awareness and understanding of spiritual truths, practical training, knowledge and experience. It is not something achieved overnight, still less is it something gained in a purely academic atmosphere. For years Colin had wanted to open a college where men and women, in a family setting and atmosphere, could learn to minister in Holy Spirit power and faith, with discipleship and servanthood as prime requisites. Such a place would preserve the distinctives of sound biblical teaching, but would have an additional dimension: training for 'ministries that would be effective in the life and power of the kingdom'.[2] Now that vision seemed about to be translated into reality.

During the months before the deal was finalised fundamental lessons of faith and discipleship were learned. Bob records the marvellously varied ways in which the deposit for Roffey Place came in, though it was a close-run thing:

Time was running out since this was the final day before the deposit fell due. At first business next morning we needed to pay fifty seven thousand pounds if the deal was to go ahead. The phone rang. It was about fifteen minutes before the close of business. The voice at the other end was that of Maureen Budgen who had become a Christian only a few months earlier in the kitchen of my house where I was sitting. She announced to me that she had nine hundred and ninety five pounds for the deposit. I asked her where she had found it.

'Under the stairs', she said. What had happened was that Maureen and her husband had been helping a friend clear out her house. She must have been a bit of a hoarder because under the stairs they found a whole load of rubbish that had to be thrown out. Amongst all this stuff was an old shoe box and in the shoe box was nine hundred and ninety five pounds in old pound notes! Nobody knew if they were legal tender, but when they rang a building society they discovered that they could be traded in. The Lord had provided just the right amount at the eleventh hour plus fifty nine minutes. I sat at the kitchen table and felt quite weak. We were now in a position to take the next, but from the human point of view the riskiest, step, to put down the deposit and enter into contract with the RSPCA. Any mistakes from this point on would be expensive ones, a point which we were to prove in fact.

It is tempting to write this and perhaps to read it as though this is all that happened. This is the skeleton. Words will never describe the passion of faith, that feeling that is a

> mixture of assurance and intensity as you become aware that something big is on the move. It is something that is beyond your own capacity and it requires resources that stretch far beyond human abilities.[3]

The payment of the deposit was merely the starting-point, for within eight weeks the remainder of the money had to be found. Many people gave generously, even sacrificially, but as the deadline grew nearer, there were few signs of the financial break-through necessary to the whole project. In stark monetary terms, £300,000 had come in towards the cost of Roffey Place; but almost the same amount was still required. That first sum had been collected over a period of four months, now just four days remained for the second £300,000. Furthermore, two dates for completion had already been and gone.

Bob remained convinced that the fellowship was meant to have Roffey Place. At this juncture Colin's faith came powerfully into the equation. From the very outset of the project Colin, like Bob, believed that God wanted the Fellowship to have a college, and he knew that God could supply the necessary resources; but that is scarcely faith. Colin does not minimise his dilemma, his *lack* of faith as he perceived it:

> I believed that he *would* supply the money; but that is not faith either. It is hope to believe that something will happen in the future. Faith says it has already happened, even if you have no visible evidence to substantiate your confidence.

> When Jesus taught His disciples to pray with faith, He told them: 'Therefore I tell you, whatever you ask for in prayer, believe that you have received it, and it will be yours' (Mark 11:24).

> *Believe that you have received it*. I believed my heavenly Father could supply the necessary money, that He would do so; but I did not believe I had received it.

> When you are not in a position of faith you can either shrug your shoulders and say that this cannot be the will of God, or

101

you can seek Him for the faith you need. The former course is actually unbelief. I had to begin my seeking by confessing my unbelief and asking for God's forgiveness.

He usually uses our times of seeking Him to sort out several issues in our lives, and I experienced a prolonged time of repentance lasting about two hours.[4]

While in Singapore he felt constrained to repent of his double-mindedness. This was followed by his receiving a direct message from God:

(God) said to me: 'Colin, I give you a million dollars.' Now faith comes from hearing God. Immediately I knew God had given the faith I needed. I was up from my knees and dancing around my hotel room with joy, praising God for His generosity.

I could not see the money, but it was as if it had already dropped on to the bed. I could go back to England and tell the others in the fellowship, 'The Lord has given me a million dollars.' That encouraged others in their faith. In Scripture, leaders are to give an example of faith for others to follow.[5]

After receiving this word from God Colin left for an extensive ministry tour in Australia, during which time he continued to praise God for the million dollars he had been assured. Several months elapsed, the million dollars were still outstanding, and he again left for a ministry trip to Australia. This is what happened next:

On the day before the money was due I telephoned home, but was told the money had not arrived. However, everyone was at peace, confident the Lord had the whole matter in hand. I also was given peace by the Lord, although I felt a tremendous sense of responsibility. It seemed we had laid our whole ministry on the line.

The other elders had to tell the vendors we did not have

all the money, but were praying for it! They did not share our faith in prayer, but we had good relationships with them during the negotiations over the property, and they offered to delay completion for a further month. That had to be the final deadline.[6]

However, on his journey home from Australia to England Colin stopped off for twenty-four hours in Singapore, the city where he had heard directly from God regarding the million dollars. What occurred there surprised even Colin:

> Some friends had invited my companions and me to dinner before driving us to the airport. At the end of the meal, my friend asked me how the college project was going. I said we were really on the faith rack, needing £300,000 by the following Friday.
>
> To my astonishment he said that his bank would wire the money to our bank so that we would have the money in time to complete the purchase.
>
> Three hundred thousand pounds is one million dollars of the currency of that nation![7]

On October 7th, 1983, the legal formalities were completed and the college opened its doors for the first batch of students in January 1984.

Some important lessons

Roffey Place Christian Training Centre began with a clear-cut vision in the hearts of Colin and Bob. Their working together in the same Fellowship was a catalyst to action and determined, faithful prayer. They stood together when difficulties emerged, including the failure to complete transactions on two of the stipulated dates. Their experiences tempered and honed their faith in God, on the one hand, and their resolution, on the other hand. They learned to rely on God and his munificence in fresh ways which will always be fixed points of reference for them as long as they live.

However, the vision for Roffey Place as a centre for ministering in the power of the Holy Spirit would have remained a mirage, had not the initial vision been accompanied by revelation. As Bob Gordon rightly says:

> True men of faith are those who learn in the midst of the struggle to wait for a word from the Lord. It may be that this word will come directly through Scripture or by another impression as the Holy Spirit bears witness within our own spirit what the will of the Father is for the situation. What happens is that this word from God encounters the burden within our heart and an intermix begins to take place as the heat of waiting and prayer is applied. The word works on the problem and the outcome is that the victory of faith is achieved in a deep internal way long before perhaps it will be seen in practical terms by other people.
>
> This produces a confidence of faith which is the outcome of the inner struggle before God.[8]

The victory of faith was not easily achieved, in fact for both men it involved a struggle. In Bob's case he endured loneliness and solitude:

> One lesson learned this last year was that God develops within us such a sense of purpose that it often threatens to overwhelm us. It cuts us off from other people, but that sense of purpose drives us into faith because the more we experience it, the more we realise that it will never be achieved unless the Lord does some marvellous things. It can be terribly frustrating when other people don't seem to share that sense of purpose or when they attempt to deviate your interest on to more passing considerations. My experience is that men of true faith live with faith issues before their eyes all the time and find it difficult when their attention is drawn away to something that may be very legitimate but, in the light of the issue in hand, will seem completely trivial.[9]

For Colin it meant acknowledging that he did not have the faith for the sum of £600,000. His predicament was a straightforward one: the Fellowship did not have this sort of money when making the offer for Roffey Place, but he was confident that it was quite definitely the property God wanted them to use as a college. In the event, their offer was accepted (although there were a number of higher ones) precisely because they were the only ones offering cash. As he laconically says, 'You need to be sure of your guidance from God before taking such a step of faith.'[10] Though sure of his guidance, Colin had never been involved with such a vast sum of money previously. Quite simply, God worked a miracle in freeing the total asking price for Roffey Place.

For Colin the experience that came to a conclusion with the purchase of Roffey Place confirmed ten fundamental biblical principles about faith, which he would sum up as follows: faith is born of vision; faith is a basic operative factor in the kingdom of God; faith is much more than hope; faith is an attitude; faith accepts that in many situations God *is* the only answer; faith grows and develops; faith is an activity; faith and experience are inextricably linked.

A recurring stress in his preaching and teaching is that faith is not what a person believes when engaged in the activity of prayer. It is a fixed attitude to the whole of life, to the successes, the problems and the difficulties, however complex and distressing the latter may be. 'Jesus does not promise,' he asserts, 'that our lives will be free of problems; but He promises that as we pray with faith, we shall see God overcoming them for us.'[11] He adds: 'Faith reduces the size of the mountains. The bigger God is in our hearts, the smaller the mountain will seem.'[12]

He also has a great deal to say in his books about the relationship between faith and experience:

'But it doesn't work! There have been occasions when I have

prayed and God hasn't done what I have asked. And I do have faith in God.'

There is no point in having our heads in a cloud of spiritual unreality. If the words that Jesus speaks are true, then they can be tested by experience and found to be true! The difficulty is that often there seems to be a confrontation between the words of Jesus and our experience. When that happens, which is true?

The problem is not so clear-cut as that. The confrontation is not really between what Jesus says and our experience. It is between 'faith' and our experience. God's promises will *never* fail, when they are believed. Believing His words means expecting those promises to be fulfilled.

There are many occasions when we honestly think that we are believing and expecting God to do what Jesus means by this word 'faith'. There can be a great difference between our ideas of 'faith' and His teaching about it. It isn't that we need to have *more* faith, but the right kind.[13]

Faith, then, to Colin is not a feeling, rather an activity. In his view, faith expresses itself in what the individual Christian says and does because, as Jesus says, from the overflow of the heart the mouth speaks. Colin comments, 'If there is faith in your heart, your mouth will proclaim that faith, and your actions will declare it.'

Colin sees an apt illustration of this in the life of our Lord when he heard that his great friend Lazarus was sick.

His immediate reaction was one of faith: 'This sickness will not end in death' (John 11:4). This is His faith reaction to the news. The enemy might want to steal the life of His beloved friend through sickness, but he will not be allowed to prevail. This is a statement of faith, and of godly indignation!

Because there is faith in His heart, Jesus does not hurry to the scene. With His eyes of faith He sees Lazarus being raised long before the event. It is four days before He arrives at the tomb. Each of His actions demonstrates the reality of His faith. 'Take away the stone,' he said (John 11:38). What would be the point of saying this unless He expected a miracle?

He is concerned to see God glorified: 'This sickness will not end in death. No, it is for God's glory so that God's Son may be glorified through it' (John 11:4). 'Did I not tell you that if you believed, you would see the glory of God?' (John 11:40).

He wants to see His Father glorified in the situation – Satan's seeming triumph will be turned to defeat. His Father's glory will be reflected in the Son as He proceeds with faith.

He stands before the tomb and prays: 'Father, I thank you that you have heard me. I knew that you always hear me, but I said this for the benefit of the people standing here, that they may believe that you sent me' (John 11:41–2).

This is prayer with faith. Jesus knows His Father always hears Him. He believes He has received His answer before there is anything to show for such confidence. The way in which He prays is an example to all those around.

Then He speaks to the 'mountain' with a word of authority: 'Lazarus, come out!' (John 11:43). And he does![14]

Faith is not merely an academic concept divorced from the realities of daily living, and the acquiring of Roffey Place confirmed this principle abundantly. So, by October 1983, the Bethany Fellowship had a college in addition to the operation based on The Hyde. How would the running and organising of Roffey work out in practice? This question could only be guessed at when the first students, including two of Colin's children, Claire and Clive, enrolled in January 1984.

The objectives of Roffey Place

An equally important issue concerned the college's aims and intentions. The aim of Roffey Place as a Christian college was to disciple men and women (particularly those involved in ministry and leadership) 'into the deeper ways of God through the work of the Holy Spirit'; and to equip them to understand 'the principles of ministering in the power of the Holy Spirit'.

From the start there were to be marked differences between Roffey Place and other more traditional Bible colleges, where the primary emphasis was often overwhelmingly academic. Examinations did not feature in the curriculum, and there was no attempt to obtain 'qualifications'. Rather the emphasis would be placed on building faith in people, encouraging them in the practical application of biblical truths, consistent and regular Bible study and prayer time, plus opportunities for ministry in the sense of preaching, leading worship, participating in house groups, going on missions in various parts of the country and, occasionally, abroad.

Naturally it was hoped that people would develop at Roffey in their understanding of the Christian faith, their personal devotion to, and relationship with, God, their ability to relate to other men and women in a meaningful way, their concern for the outcasts and poor in society. In the latter case the lectures of David Brown were extremely powerful and motivated many students to take seriously the task of the church in reaching such people.

The courses at Roffey were designed to be flexible: people could enrol for one or two or three terms, depending on their home circumstances, arrangements with employers or financial and other considerations. To achieve the objectives alluded to above, the schedule at Roffey contained five main components: lectures, group activities, worship, practical service and missions.

The lectures inevitably differed from term to term, but a not untypical term might contain in-depth studies of an Old Testament book, a New Testament epistle, the prophetic phenomena, the gifts of the Spirit, the concept of authority and leadership, and the idea of servanthood.

Group activities might involve house groups, prayer triplets (usually early in the morning), or worship times. These occasions encouraged a sense of fellowship and of life together, but also gave the students the opportunity to operate in the gifts of the Spirit. Each day at Roffey began with a time of praise and worship, the conviction being that any preaching or application of the Word should be based on a platform of worship and adoration.

Practical service included washing up after meals, cooking and gardening, and help with the upkeep of the college's fabric. The last two of these were usually carried out on Wednesday afternoons when no formal lectures took place.

Missions could take place at weekends, or for more extended periods, and were invaluable in giving the students the opportunity to observe people like Colin, Bob, Michael Barling and Charles Sibthorpe teaching, preaching and leading teams: a sort of in-service training with the experts. On some of these missions students would go into the local schools and colleges with the message of the gospel. These times were not always easy or comfortable for them, as the school children often asked difficult and even hostile questions which required wisdom, common sense and intelligence: students frequently found that religious cliches were simply not acceptable to the inquirers; still less were they able to hide behind woolly or waffly answers!

The objectives of the college were clear-cut, but how did they work out in practice? One student wrote to me as follows:

> My time at Roffey was extremely rewarding, in a number of different ways.
>
> First, I was able, because free from the demands of my daily profession, to spend time in a relaxed way in reading the Bible, praying and meditating. This I had not been able to do previously because my life was very definitely activity-orientated: I thus learned the need for reflection and meditation – simply 'to be' before God without the pressure of preaching, organising meetings and such like.

It was therefore a time of refreshing for me personally, emotionally and spiritually. In a very real sense my spiritual batteries were re-charged. I saw the benefit of this when I returned to my church after completing the course.

Second, the atmosphere was exciting: an air of expectancy pervaded the whole college that was the product of faith in God, the belief that 'nothing was impossible for Him'.

Third, the presence of men like Colin Urquhart and Bob Gordon, who had established international ministries, was an additional encouragement to faith. Their example and teaching built confidence in the students, many of whom were eager – and indeed motivated – to follow their example.

Fourth, some of the 'guest' lecturers and preachers, for example, David Pawson and Campbell Macalpine, as well as visitors from abroad, were men of stature and extremely varied experience. David's lectures, in particular, were a model of thorough, painstaking preparation, biblical wisdom and enlightened intelligence.

Fifth, close fellowship and friendship amongst the students. Like students in any establishment, they talked endlessly on a vast number of subjects, sharing their failures, successes, etc. Solid, in some cases life-long friendships were forged in a place where God was honoured and revered.

My time at Roffey Place confirmed within me personally principles of faith, holiness and discipleship that I had only ever seriously considered after the baptism in the Holy Spirit.

I had an encounter with God at Roffey, for which I'll always be grateful.

David Hill, who now pastors a church in Wantage, Oxfordshire, spent three terms at the college, and his perception of his time there was conveyed to me in a letter as follows:

Colin Urquhart was used as a channel by God in two separate incidents that changed the whole direction of my life.

The first was when he was the main speaker at a meeting in Oxford Town Hall. Mid-way through his message Colin stopped and said that the Lord had laid on his heart a scripture which was specific for a person at the meeting. The Word was the exact scripture the Lord had given my wife and me the previous week, but we had asked the Lord for a confirmation before acting upon it. We asked God to re-affirm His word through Colin, as he, at that time, had never met us and was therefore an independent and impartial witness. From that Word we moved to the village, where I now pastor a church, although at that stage it was some six to seven years down the road. Also at the same meeting the person who is now in eldership with me was healed of sinus problems.

It was also while attending another meeting that God, through Colin, confirmed that I should spend a period of reflection and study at Roffey Place. I was convinced that God was calling me to some form of study but until that meeting I had no firm conviction or confirmation of its location.

What were my lasting impressions of Colin from my time at Roffey? Well, on the positive side, he was a man of great personal faith; he was a man of prayer. I knew, from the simplicity and straightforwardness of his faith that it was *real*. By simplicity, I mean that he took the truth of the Word of God, believed it and implemented it, and it worked. Because of his own uncomplicated beliefs his lectures were always concise and a direct exposition of the Bible, especially those on faith and healing. Personally I found them both faith building and challenging, with a desire to see the reality of those teachings become effective in my own experience. However, I know for some of the students the gap between the Word and the way Colin took hold of these truths, and the experiences in their own lives, was a difficult one to bridge. This was especially so on the subject of healing. For many their personal views and experiences seemed so different from the teaching on healing, which wasn't helped by the death of David Watson at that time. I thank God that I became a Christian under a man of God greatly used in praying for the sick and I had seen and experienced

111

God's healing. So I found Colin's lectures a challenge, not a stumbling-block, as I sought to bring my experience into line with God's Word rather than God's Word being changed to match my experience.

Colin was a man who spoke faith into every situation. Yet despite this upfront show of faith and the reality of it working in his own life, he was never someone to whom you could draw close. There always seemed to be a protective layer around him that very few, if any, seemed to be able to penetrate. Whether this was a deliberate shield or not, I was never sure, but this apparent distancing was sad because much is to be learned from drawing alongside the great men of faith, while knowing more about their personal walk enables you to see the depths in God.

I appreciated my time at Roffey for many reasons, and will always be grateful for that year in my life. It was there my faith developed and matured; and perhaps the most precious thing was the way my personal relationship with the Lord became so much more intimate. I will always be grateful to Colin for his part in my spiritual development.

Problems and difficulties

A college – be it Christian or secular – is a living, developing organism and, inevitably, encounters difficulties and tensions. Roffey Place was no different. From my own experiences as a student there, imbalances were apparent in several areas, reflecting an early stage of the college's development. Things are very different today. Not only, as Colin points out, is the community now enjoying a reviving move of the Spirit, but the whole college is run on different principles.

In the early days, the standard of lecturing was variable, which led to frustration, especially for those with previous academic training. A number of the lecturers viewed genuine questions of enquiry with suspicion and, some saw them as an affront to their position and integrity. Honest questioning is an important part of any college, and in this sense Roffey Place was a disappointment to some people.

Another problem was that inadequate provision was made for the pastoral direction of the students. Many people had unresolved issues in their lives – personal, emotional, spiritual, psychological – which required disciplined, skilful and regular counselling. This was simply not available to them. In the early years of Roffey, the very idea of 'inner healing' was discounted because Colin's perceived view of it was a minimal one, and so students tended to hide their dilemmas from 'the authorities', resorting instead to sharing their problems with interested friends who then gave what advice and counselling help they could. In some cases, this *ad hoc* arrangement was beneficial, in others it was less satisfactory. There was also the feeling – not entirely correct – that Bob Gordon was far too busy with his teaching and ministry to give sustained help and direction to those with serious problems in their lives.

In the third place, students were inadequately discipled. While the notion of discipling men and women for greater usefulness in God's kingdom was high on the college's agenda, the reality was very different, according to a number of former students. Where men and women had come from a life of violence, or immorality, or drug addiction, or drunkenness, for example, what they needed was an ongoing, preferably one-to-one, course in the meaning and significance of discipleship. Instead these people were often asked to give their testimonies and minister, when they were not prepared for it.

Discipleship training would have built important foundations of knowledge, integrity and perseverance in their lives. Instead they imbibed a sense of self-importance which if left uncorrected in the light of the Word of God, was potentially disastrous, and indeed proved to be so in a limited number of cases.

But these observations need to be qualified and balanced.

The overall variable standard of lecturing was inevitable given the variety of people invited by the college to participate in the lecturing scheme. Also, it was valuable to listen to people with real experience of life, in which they had been signally used by God, and whose examples might profitably be imitated. Such instances compensated for a lack of purely technical lecturing skills, or external polish.

In the second place, while the overall pastoral care was inadequate, it often meant that the younger students would approach older and more experienced students for help and counsel. This sort of help and assistance was almost invariably forthcoming, much of it both considerate and prayerful. In such circumstances, friendships were formed which have lasted far beyond the time at Roffey.

It is also fair to say that a large number of the students did not require lengthy discipling as they were part of fellowships or churches where such an approach was securely built into the system, and they were balanced in their faith.

Colin's ministry outside the college was thriving. What, then, was his rôle at Roffey Place?

Roffey Place and Colin

As Principal, Bob Gordon had overall responsibility for the college's direction, ethos and framework of lectures, and he brought to it his characteristically dynamic flair and considerable teaching skills. He says this about Colin's relationship with what went on:

> Colin obviously brought a great deal to Roffey. In the first instance we shared together in its purchase and foundation. That was a great experience which contained many lessons of faith.
>
> His teaching was a central part of Roffey although this

114

proved difficult in practice. Increasingly, I think, Colin felt excluded from Roffey. It was sometimes practically difficult to put a curriculum together to fit with Colin's many ministry movements. But maybe this was part of our different viewpoints.

Others have confirmed to me their disappointment that Colin seemed to be absent from Roffey for large tracts of time. This was primarily due to the demands of his itinerant ministry, at home and abroad, but it meant that the students were not able to benefit from his deep experience of God, his skills as a preacher, his 'healing' ministry, and the direct influence that a day-to-day involvement in the life of the college would have meant. 'Cheated' would perhaps be too strong a word to describe the reactions of students to Colin's many absences from Roffey, but many felt sorely disappointed that they could not profit from his obviously rich and diverse experience of God. To fit him into the lecturing curriculum became increasingly problematical, for Bob, but Colin does not feel that it contributed to the unspoken tensions between himself and Bob.

There is a world of difference between identifying a problem and finding a solution for it, and neither Colin nor Bob, both strong and determined men, found a way to bridge the gap on this potentially contentious issue. Others at Roffey could see the problem all too clearly, but felt incapable of attempting to rectify it in a manner that would be mutually pleasing and acceptable. An uneasy truce therefore prevailed, the one certainty (all were agreed) being that, eventually, the situation would have to be clarified.

1984–89 were testing years for Colin. This was so for a variety of reasons, all connected with the work, outreach and personalities of the Bethany Fellowship.

Tensions at Abbot's Leigh and The City

The vision for Abbot's Leigh (a drug rehabilitation and discipling centre) and The City (a cinema which could be used as a spearhead for evangelism) was essentially David Brown's. This work started out under the aegis of the Bethany Fellowship, with Colin supporting David in his concern for those people with very serious personal problems. Once the work got going it developed very quickly: too quickly, in fact, so much so that Colin and his fellow elders were marginalised. There were also financial pressures at The City. David devised various ambitious schemes for a financial rescue package which the elders felt were, at best, ill-advised, at worst, foolish and imprudent. Between them Bob Gordon, Michael Barling and Charles Sibthorpe had had considerable experience of the business world, but David, they felt, was not open to their direction and guidance.

The situation was highly charged, with currents of tension reverberating within the Fellowship. The result was that the ventures at Abbot's Leigh and The City became more detached from their foundations in the Fellowship, and a separate charity was formed. Too much had been undertaken too quickly. The trustees of the new trust decided that the two properties should be sold.

In retrospect, it is clear that David acted in good faith and with enthusiasm, but while he was a brilliant deputy, he was not skilled or gifted to lead a work. He had definite pastoral and teaching gifts, but was not equipped to work in isolation from the elders. The situation was exacerbated by the fact that David had financial backers to buy the various properties which, in a sense, were purchased too easily. A faith-work requires a battle, an element absent from the purchase of Abbot's Leigh and The City.

Colin felt David's departure very keenly. This was hardly surprising as David was converted in Luton and had been with

Colin since the early days at The Hyde. Initially David's ministry – both pastorally and in preaching – developed extremely well, but the later tensions between them were not resolved by David's rapid departure from the Fellowship. Re-reading the relevant sections in *Faith for the Future* and *Out of the Melting Pot* is deeply poignant, even today. In his book, Colin recounts the deep love he had for David and his respect for his gifts, while Bob's book speaks with enthusiasm about the work at Abbot's Leigh. 1984 was a deeply painful year for Colin and the Fellowship, and the loss of David, with his prophetic vision for the poor in society, has meant that a gap exists in the overall work of the Fellowship because no one else has captured his vision for the under-privileged to the same extent.

Adjustments within the Fellowship

By 1986 the Bethany Fellowship had grown to about two hundred people, many of whom were actively involved in ministry, while others who lived and worked locally were part of the community in a wider sense. Such people helped with outreach, worship and evangelistic teams but were not supported financially by the community. During this year the Fellowship felt they had heard from God to leave The Hyde and establish Roffey Place not only as a college but also as a base for worship and work. It was also felt necessary to change the *name* from the 'Bethany Fellowship' to 'Kingdom Faith Ministries' because, as Bob Gordon explains,

> God had called us to move out and see the establishment of His kingdom through the proclamation of his Word in the power of His Spirit, and to issue to His people the call to radical discipleship.

Kingdom Faith Ministries was launched at the Faith '87 summer camp at Peterborough. Its declared aims were five-fold: to encourage spiritual revival in the churches of Britain and overseas; to deepen the faith of Christians; to promote true discipleship among believers; to train people for ministry in the power of the Holy Spirit; and to see the kingdom of God extended through evangelistic outreach.

As the ministry diversified and increased in momentum, many of the original Fellowship and community members left to undertake new ministry elsewhere. Thus, from August 1987, a time of change and pruning came, accompanied by the inevitable uncertainty change brings in its wake. It was not an easy time, either for Colin or his team. There were those who felt the new initiatives meant that one chapter in their lives was closing, with the obvious need to move on. As people left they were replaced by those who could develop their gifts and ministries under the new banner of Kingdom Faith Ministries.

At this time, too, another ingredient in the mix was the King's Coach Ministry. This had grown in response to a vision given to Bob Gordon during a conference at Swanwick in 1985, for five coaches to be placed strategically throughout Britain, each with its own team, base and local identity, in order to present the Gospel to men and women who would not otherwise have an opportunity to hear it. The first coach had begun to operate in August 1986, so by 1987 the work as a whole was growing in size, impetus and confidence. It is a work that continues powerfully to this day, though between 1987–80 it was not without its pressure on the relationship between Colin and Bob.

Parting from Bob Gordon

It had been apparent almost from the time they started working together that Colin and Bob had their own agendas, plans and visions. It was clear to their close colleagues that friction would arise between them. The most obvious area for contention was the division of what might be called 'preaching slots' at, say, big occasions like the summer camps.

Colin was still looked upon as the 'leader' of the work in an overall sense, so that, not surprisingly, Bob felt that his wings were being clipped, while Colin, some erroneously contend, felt threatened by someone like Bob with his great abilities as a teacher of the Word of God. Elements of insecurity prevailed in both men, which again were apparent to those working in close proximity to them. It was a dilemma in which it was possible to feel sympathy for both men in what became an impossible situation. The situation was complicated even more when it became clear that the King's Coaches were not operating under the overall authority or direction of the elders of Kingdom Faith Ministries, perhaps the most clear-cut example of a private agenda in Bob's work. This fact may have caused Colin to feel let down by Bob.

Eventually, as is well known, Colin and Bob parted company after quite a lengthy period when opposing postures were assumed by the two teams of helpers surrounding the two men. What began as a breakdown in communication led to a broken relationship, culminating in a parting of the ways. The inter-related reasons were outlined in a letter to me by Bob:

> On the surface, it became necessary at a practical level. Roffey Place was the only viable central unit of the Bethany Fellowship left. The City led by David Brown and The Hyde where Charles Sibthorpe held the Leaders' Weeks had both closed and Roffey had become the central focus of the Fellowship's life. In some ways this stood in tension with the daily life of the college. With the growth of the work and the felt need of Colin for a true work-base Roffey became too small for the whole work.
>
> Another factor was the growth of my own ministry. The advent of the King's Coach and its subsequent rapid growth placed other strains not only on the space at Roffey but on its direction and ethos. This is quite understandable and, even before the parting suddenly came, we were engaged on

119

long discussions about opening another centre in proximity to Roffey. The Prayer Letters of the time reflect this fact.

Underneath there were other factors, I am sure. But these were never elucidated. These were related to perceptions of ministry and perhaps theological issues, but that is not a word that surfaced too often. From my point of view this was not a problem because I felt that part of Roffey's raison d'être was to provide a context of exploration and discussion about issues. In the end the decision was effectively made for us to leave and that was that.

Obviously, this was one of the most painful times of my life, but not because of profound disagreement with Colin. My disagreements were functional, that is, on how the issues were or were not handled, rather than personal. It was painful for two main reasons. One, because in Colin I had found a spiritual peer who also taught me a lot and with whom I had perceived a deep spiritual partnership. My feeling is that Colin perceived the growth of my own team as a threat to that and maybe in some ways it was. It's difficult to be objective. Two, my heart was in the growth and success of Roffey. I saw it as a place of growing maturity which would serve as a crucial centre in facing the growing challenges and changes within the renewal scene. Maybe I got it wrong there but, in the end, it became clear it was a different perception from Colin's.

Colin has steadfastly refused to comment on the reasons for the separation with Bob.

I regarded Bob as a fine teacher of the Word. I enjoyed listening to him teach and in flowing together with him in ministry. This was never a threat and bears no relation to the reasons for Bob's departure from Kingdom Faith. I know some of my failings, I know I have made mistakes and openly confessed to them, but being of a jealous disposition towards those working with me is not one of them.

Colin felt that Bob's ambition in God was not being tempered by caution or by concern for others, including himself. He did believe, though, that God wanted the two men to go different ways, but that the whole thing went wrong because it wasn't conducted in God's way. He also feels that Satan wanted to destroy both ministries. Communication between Colin and Caroline and Bob and Hilda broke down, and it was an immensely painful and distressing period for both men and their families. Charles Sibthorpe had warned Colin in December 1986 that Bob had his own plans for the future direction of the work, so that in the end a feeling of *déjà vu* dominated the thinking of those colleagues and friends at Roffey Place who watched, with concern and in some cases anguish, as what might realistically be called a 'power struggle' worked through to its conclusion.

Since their parting, however, both Colin and Bob have grown in their own ministries. The work of the King's Coaches has developed significantly, spreading as far as New Zealand. Colin's ministry, too, has come to a place of greater peace and he has had the freedom to shape Roffey Place and Kingdom Faith Ministries in the way he wants it to develop. Two strong and determined men, both with natural and supernatural giftings from God, have been able to proceed in the way they desired. It is possible to assert that God has worked 'for the good' of both Colin *and* Bob. Both men have a basic integrity, and their dilemma was an intractable one which could only be resolved, given the complexity of life and ministries at Roffey, by working separately from each other.

As Bob rightly says, 'We need to say in the end that the Lord used all this to bring about the best.' What it also means is that Colin and Bob are reaching and influencing people who perhaps might not be reached had they stayed together preserving, as it were, an uneasy truce. Hopefully both have learned, at a profound level, that the work of God does not, ultimately, depend upon them: the battle, after all, is the Lord's. It is a salutary lesson for all concerned.

10

THE PREACHER

Any understanding of Colin Urquhart's remarkable ministry would be incomplete without an assessment of his preaching. It is to an examination of this fundamental part of his many-faceted work that we now turn.

The call to preach

The idea of standing before a congregation to preach held no appeal for Colin in his youth; indeed, like many a choirboy, Colin's main preoccupation during the sermons was to amuse himself by nudging the head of the person in front of him. At that time, preaching seemed to him a 'very precarious business' – even more so since in his local church a large wooden sounding board was suspended from the ceiling over the pulpit on three wires!

Yet, when his Vicar mentioned the subject of ordination, something stirred deep within him and, somehow he sensed 'a rightness, an inevitability, in what was being suggested'. The fact of God's call on his life did nothing to quell his feelings of human inadequacy: he was fearful and self-conscious.

During the early years of his ministry he faced two particular areas in which his own inadequacy was all too apparent, but in which he discovered God's willingness to empower and enable him by the Holy Spirit to achieve things that were not possible in purely human strength and resources. Colin says this:

> The first of these issues concerned healing. I had not been trained at college to heal the sick; yet the Lord confronted me with the gospel command, 'Heal the sick.' He began to teach me that he was prepared to enable that if I was prepared to trust Him. Another such area was preaching. I was not brought up in an evangelical tradition and therefore did not see preaching, although part of my ministry in its early years, as a means of drawing people to definite commitment to Jesus Christ, to conversion experience or new birth. But it was a necessary part of my function as an ordained priest.[1]

In each of his three parishes, changes occurred in his preaching method and in his understanding of what preaching was meant to achieve. In Letchworth, he realised that preaching wasn't simply a matter of preparing a sermon in the study and making copious notes. He began to understand that 'instead of me speaking for God, He needed to speak *through* me'. Alongside this fresh insight was Colin's willingness to trust God to use him as a vehicle. Another, in many ways more fundamental, change took place, too: he now prepared for his sermons in a totally different way. He explains: 'I no longer prepared sermons . . . I prepared *myself* to preach.' This preparation was in prayer, in waiting on God, in being with Him, and humbling himself before God.

By the time he moved to St Hugh's, Lewsey, this was his usual method of preaching. He had already grown accustomed to the fact that he 'would preach something under the inspiration of the Spirit and discover the same truths in Scripture afterwards. It was not so much a question of my being able to reveal the Scriptures to the people, as the Spirit revealing the Scriptures to me and the people.' This is, of course, consistent with the promise of Jesus that the Spirit would guide us into all truth (John 16:13).

At Luton, too, he learned one important lesson from the very beginning: 'If God speaks to His people, they must be given time in which to respond – immediately. That response involves faith in what God has said and repentance so that His life may be appropriated!' The conviction that preaching under the anointing of the Spirit inevitably leads to faith and repentance became a fixed principle in his approach:

> I would never preach without giving adequate time for response. The result was that we witnessed the signs that the Scriptures promise will accompany the preaching of the gospel. Lives were transformed, people were set free from bondages, and bodies, emotions and relationships were healed. The sermon did not need to be on the subject of healing for healing to take place. That issue might not even have been mentioned. It was enough to preach the gospel in the power of the Spirit for the works of the Spirit to be demonstrated.[2]

Thus it was that Colin discovered at Luton the need for a two-fold ministry: inspirational preaching and anointed preaching. He explains further:

> Both were utterly dependent on the working of the Holy Spirit. I know beyond any questioning that what was happening was the result of the Holy Spirit speaking and working through me. Consequently it seemed that those events had nothing to do with me personally. And yet I was aware of my responsibility to be in the right place with God so that he could speak and work through me in the way he desired. Although I no longer wrote my sermons I was diligent in spending time with the Word of God every day. Since the beginning of my ministry an important part of my daily devotions was spent waiting on God and listening to him. These times of reading and listening were exciting because revelation was happening every day as God's truths were spoken to my heart by the Holy Spirit. When you receive revelation you are able to impart revelation to others.

God had a unique thing to do on every occasion. If I was trusting the Holy Spirit to speak through me and believing I would be the Lord's mouthpiece, then we as a congregation could never settle into a rut. God would speak to His people as a whole and specifically to individuals as well. In this way the Lord would confront us with the particular issues He wanted to deal with and give vision as to where He wanted to lead us.[3]

So it was that, gradually, Colin's whole life became a preparation for what would happen when he stood on his feet to proclaim the Word of God:

This means that not only my study of the Word but my times of prayer, my waiting upon God, my listening to Him and even my seeking to walk in righteousness, living out my life in Christ Jesus, are all a preparation for preaching. But like St Paul I do not believe I have fully preached the gospel unless I see the evidence of God's power afterwards, unless I see the evidence of the signs and wonders that are promised in the Scriptures.[4]

Principles for preachers

Colin identifies four primary requirements for preachers. First, boldness. By this he means the speaking out of what God has already given a preacher to communicate to the congregation. This, he contends, is as normative for those who are by nature fearful or self-conscious as for those who are naturally bold and courageous. The New Testament features the example of the disciples who prayed for increasing boldness in their preaching, and so, Colin believes, should all modern preachers.

Second, graciousness and love. This has to do with the way a preacher says what God has given him. Where the message is uncomfortable or hard-hitting, a preacher must speak with love and grace, not in a condemning or dictatorial manner. Before each sermon Colin asks God for a real love for the people, but on one aspect he is most emphatic: 'Anybody who is going to have a faithful preaching ministry has to put his love for God before his love for man and acceptance by the people. He only truly loves the people by declaring to them the full counsel of God, whether that is popular or not.'[5]

A third principle of preaching is that of authority. This is not something a preacher can create for himself, and Colin distinguishes it sharply from authoritarianism. Authority, he believes, is the product of submission to God's own authority in a preacher's life, while authoritarianism is apparent when God-given authority is missing:

> The more fully submitted a Christian is to the Lord, the more he or she will speak with authority. In practice this means that the preacher has to live his message or he will speak without conviction. Much preaching is mind-centred and therefore bears little fruit, even though it may be true in content. The one who speaks from the heart will communicate to the hearts of his listeners, and that will call for a response from them. If the preacher has already been dealt with by God over the issue about which he is speaking, he will speak not only with conviction but also with authority about loving others if he lives out that commitment in his own personal life.[6]

The fourth principle is faith. The Bible teaches that everything that is not of faith is sin, which applies equally to preaching as to any other activity of the Christian faith. 'Faith,' says Colin, 'comes from hearing the words of Christ proclaimed', which of course is almost a paraphrase of Romans 10:17. Faith is the very antithesis of human knowledge or understanding, still less is it engendered by a preacher reflecting on life and his own experience of it, however valuable in human terms. Colin's fundamental conviction is that a preacher's rôle is to direct his listeners to the revelation of God's Word, and to personal faith in Him. He also says this:

> Christians need to understand more fully who God is, what He has done for them in Jesus, and what He has made them because they belong to Him. So the preacher needs to live in this revelation himself. He will not be effective in imparting it to others unless he does so. How can a preacher expect his congregation to live by the scriptural principles of faith, if he constantly speaks of failure and defeat and lives in an aura of despair? He will not build faith in others by criticising or condemning them, but only by enabling them to see themselves as God sees them, living in Christ Jesus as a new creation. The old has passed away and the new has come. They are being led in His triumphal procession. They are blessed with every spiritual blessing in heaven, every need of theirs is met through the riches that are theirs in Christ, and by His stripes they are healed. When the preacher lives faith, he speaks faith and encourages faith in others. Then the people can approach every situation with faith, knowing they live in the victory Christ has already won.[7]

It isn't a case of living the Word of God perfectly – no one does that – rather, that true liberty in preaching is the result of putting into practice the teaching of Scripture. Nor is it simply doctrinal correctness which often leads to spiritual aridity, or academic training without the reality of the living Christ in a person's life. The paramount need is, in Colin's phrase, for 'heart conviction', which means allowing Christ, as He told His disciples, to live *in* a person and in allowing His Word to control his heart, mind and spirit.

It is clear, too, that Colin is captivated by the thrill of preaching, what Martyn Lloyd-Jones in *Preaching and Preachers* calls 'the romance of preaching'. Colin describes it thus:

> When I stand up to preach something happens inside me, the words are there and they simply pour out until the inspiration comes to an end. Then is the time to stop. If I try to continue when the inspiration has ended, there is

no longer any authority in what I say. When you are used
to preaching under anointing you sure notice the difference
if you speak without it. Anointing has nothing to do with
feelings. In my busy lifestyle which consists of travelling,
speaking, writing, and broadcasting – as well as leading a
fellowship – there are times of utter exhaustion when the
last thing I want to do is preach. Yet as soon as I am on
my feet I experience God's anointing of power. My mind
clears and as I stand there proclaiming His Word, I know
I am fulfilling His purpose for my life.[8]

Colin is at one with Lloyd-Jones, too, in stressing the centrality
of preaching for the life and witness of the Christian church.
Lloyd-Jones speaks about this in *Preaching and Preachers*: 'I
would say without any hesitation that the most urgent need in
the Christian Church today is true preaching; and as it is the
greatest and the most urgent need in the Church, it is obviously
the greatest need of the world also.'[9] Lloyd-Jones claims that
the absence of such preaching is the chief explanation of 'the
present more or less parlous condition and ineffectiveness of
the Christian Church in the world today.'[10] Like Lloyd-Jones,
Colin regrets the fact that preaching no longer occupies a central
place in the ministry of many churches, which he attributes
to 'a decline in the quality of anointed preaching'. He rightly
comments that 'many people only have a seven or eight minute
sermonette and nobody can live in the power of God's Word
on such a diet'. He goes on to say,

Today there is great hunger among God's people to hear
the Word preached under the anointing of the Holy Spirit, a
great desire to hear from God. There is a kind of evangelical
judgmentalism, when people sit back weighing and judging
everything that is said to ensure that it balances with their
own doctrinal perspective. Such congregations see little of the
move and activity of God's Spirit in power. There are others,
no less concerned for truth, who nevertheless are expecting
God to speak directly to touch their lives and to confirm His
word with power. To preach in two such congregations is as

different as chalk and cheese. In one there is a hard rigidity, in the other an openness to what is wanting and a willingness to move with Him in the power of the Spirit.[11]

Colin would argue powerfully therefore that the primary task of the church is to preach the Word of God, to declare the 'manifold wisdom of God' (Ephesians 3:8–10); and that only the church can do this. He also argues strongly for sufficient time at a meeting for both the preaching of the Word and the ministry which needs to accompany it. In fact, he sees the time of ministry after the sermons as an indispensable part of the preaching, and not an optional extra tagged on at the end. He explains why:

> People will be led in repentance, filled with the Holy Spirit and healed. We deprive the people and grieve God if we do not give Him sufficient opportunity to work in sovereign power. And if He is at work and people are being mightily blessed it does not matter how long the service lasts![12]

In other words, Colin conceives of preaching as something which deals with the *whole* person, and again it is instructive to compare his attitude with that of Lloyd-Jones:

> Preaching is that which deals with the total person, the hearer becomes involved and knows that he has been dealt with and addressed by God through this preacher. Something has taken place in him and in his experience, and it is going to affect the whole of his life.[13]

It is a process in which the preacher's whole personality is involved and this leads to an exchange between the preacher and his hearers which affects both the person imparting God's Word and those listening to it. Colin takes his preaching very seriously because he is dealing with God's truth and revelation. He is, at one and the same time, aware of the immense responsibility bestowed upon him while also experiencing the freedom and joy of the Spirit. To him, it is an enormous privilege to be called to preach, to stand between God and men and women as an ambassador for Christ, to lead people into the life and power of the Spirit. What, then, are the primary features of his preaching?

Faith

Colin Urquhart is above all things a man of faith. He desires to build solid foundations of faith in other people, and he loves to preach about faith. It is, of course, a particular and biblical faith in God which, in turn, leads to faith in His Word.

In *Anything You Ask*, Colin shows that believing God, His Word and His promises can only come about through the work of the Holy Spirit within a person. It is the rôle of the Spirit to teach and to bring to remembrance the words of Jesus (John 14:26), to declare the words of Jesus in such a way that faith is created and matured.

None of this would be possible without saving faith, a theme Colin delights in returning to in his preaching, especially the results of Jesus's death on the cross of Calvary. In *In Christ Jesus*, he explains eternal life in the context of faith:

> Jesus had to die in order that sinners could be reconciled with God. Because you have put your faith in Him and in what He did for you on the cross, you 'have eternal life in him'. You did not deserve that; you could do nothing to achieve it. *God has given you eternal life as a gift* – not because of what you are, but because of who Jesus is; not because of what you have done, but because of what He has done for you. Your eternal life is *in Him*.[14]

The results of faith are radical, and, as he frequently asserts in his preaching, they include righteousness, so that a person need not think of himself as a spiritual reject and thus unacceptable to God; knowing Christ and the ability to enjoy a personal and intimate relationship with Him; justification, which means that we are completely forgiven by Jesus who, moreover, declares that we are innocent because our guilt has been washed away by His blood; redemption, His grace bringing us out of darkness by His life; salvation, the knowledge that through Jesus we are loved, accepted and approved of by God, an understanding which leads to joy and gladness; and being born of God: when a person puts his or her faith in God he or she becomes a child of God.

Colin frequently preaches on the need for an expectant faith whereby a Christian not only acknowledges and accepts that God is almighty, but also expects Him to work in almighty ways in the circumstances of his or her life. For him, this is part of our rich inheritance in Christ: 'What is impossible without faith becomes possible with faith – so long as that faith is in God through Jesus.'

The challenge of faith is not, in Colin's view, to do with the amount of faith a person may have, but with who that faith is in. Faith must be in Jesus, and earthed in His promises, so that His ministry is ongoing in this world:

> The works of power in Jesus's life cannot be separated from His fellowship with His Father and His submission to His authority. It is God's purpose to continue the ministry of Jesus in the world through you and all other believers. How far God can do that through you will depend upon your fellowship with Him and your obedience to Him. If that was true for Jesus, it is true for you, too.[15]

Time and again in his preaching Colin returns to the following elements of faith:

The prayer of faith. A key verse is Mark 11:24, 'Therefore I tell you, whatever you ask in prayer, believe that you have received it, and it will be yours.' Colin takes the phrase 'whatever you

ask' literally: 'When you ask, you are to believe that you have
already received the answer to your prayer.' However, he adds,
'You can only believe like that, if you know that God wants to
give you that particular thing for which you ask, if the Spirit
witnesses that truth to your heart.'

The confession of faith. In *Our Rich Inheritance* Colin highlights
a five-fold confession of faith:

1 Learn to speak the Word to YOURSELF.
2 Learn to speak the Word to GOD.
3 Learn to speak the Word to SATAN.
4 Learn to speak the Word to other BELIEVERS.
5 Learn to speak the Word to the WORLD.[16]

He attached special importance to the last of these declarations:

> You are surrounded by people who do not know the Lord!
> What they need is not your opinions or philosophies, but
> the Word of God. Again, this is not a question of quoting
> repentance scriptures at them!
>
> Speaking the Word of God to them, means that you first
> ask God to give you the right word for the situation. It may
> be a word of Scripture, or a prophetic word. It may even
> be a question that God leads you to ask, which opens up
> a fruitful conversation. Whatever it is, you are sharing the
> truth of God with them and the Word will be very much a
> part of it.
>
> The promises of Scripture are not for unbelievers and you
> may have to point this out to them. You can show them
> how they can come into a relationship with Christ, whereby
> they make these promises their inheritance also. Allow Him
> to lead you, to guide you, and to put into your mouth the
> right words to speak. If you are open to the leading of the
> Holy Spirit, He will do that![17]

Acting out faith. Colin teaches that faith is not a feeling; it is an activity, and faith expresses itself in what a person says and does. In *Listen and Live*, he points to the example of Jesus when he heard that Lazarus was sick: His immediate reaction was one of faith, whereby He declared that 'This sickness will not end in death' (John 11:4). Colin insists that a Christian needs faith attitudes in his heart, and he takes the view that words and actions which do not spring from heart attitudes of faith are merely external and do not constitute real faith.

Testing of faith. Faith is tested by the various difficulties that God allows us to encounter in this world. Instead of resenting these testings, God wants us to look to Him with faith that He will carry us through. Colin declares that genuine faith believes God whatever the circumstances, indeed regardless of them. Ultimately we do not have faith in God, or love Him, because of what we can get out of Him, but because of who He is and the love He has demonstrated in Jesus.

Little faith: Colin frequently alludes to the failure of the disciples to cure an epileptic boy, after which Jesus taught them some important lessons about faith. The incident is recorded in Matthew Chapter 17, upon which Colin comments:

> Their failure was due to their little faith. And yet Jesus goes on to tell them that they only needed as much faith as a tiny seed and they would not only have been able to move this mountain, but that 'nothing will be impossible' for them. Obviously the kind of faith Jesus was referring to, was different from the faith that the disciples were exercising when they were praying with the boy.[18]

Faith-full speech: Colin teaches that a person full of positive faith will speak positive words; that is the opposite of the fear and unbelief that tends to speak negatively. The two responses lead to different results. A positive response will cause a person to look to Jesus, confident that He will not fail; while the negative response will lead to frustration, fear, dejection, even anger. The counter-balance, as always, is to store the Word of God 'in your heart so that it may be a wellspring of life' in the inner life of a person.

The shield of faith. Each person is prone to doubt which, in Colin's opinion, has three main sources: the world around us, personal unbelief and Satan, who wishes to destroy faith if he possibly can. The antidote for doubt, in every situation, is to put on the 'shield of faith' which 'can quench all the flaming darts of the evil one' (Ephesians 6:16), and Colin counsels: 'Hold on to the promises that your Father gives to you as His new covenant child, and refuse to accept any of the enemy's lies.'

Colin's preaching on faith has one supreme and over-riding aim: to bring Christians to the place of faith where they trust God absolutely, rather than being influenced by the deceptions of Satan, immediate circumstances, or the accumulated wisdom of life's experiences. As he says, 'God does not want us to reduce His word to the level of our experience; He wants our experience raised to the level of His word'; the corollary is that 'Our experience will only be raised to the level of God's word if we learn to affirm positively the truth of that word in the face of every difficulty and temptation to doubt'.[19]

The authority of Scripture

Colin's thinking is moulded by the words of Scripture. He believes, without any reservation at all, that these are God's words and, as such, are 'spirit and life' (John 6:63). So when the Holy Spirit begins to operate in a person's life these words take on a new rock-like meaning, with personal and practical relevance for that person's life: 'The words of Jesus are not only for the times in which they were spoken or when the books of the Bible were written. They are words of eternal life, of eternal meaning and significance.'[20]

Colin insists that if Christians are not depending on the words of Jesus, they are on the sand, which is disastrous, and he develops his thinking in a chapter of *Anything You Ask* entitled 'The Word':

> The sand can consist of many different things:
>
> The sand can be basing your life on the opinions of men, or your own opinions even.
>
> The sand can be believing your own ideas of God, instead of what the Bible reveals about Him.
>
> The sand can be depending upon having experiences of God. The experiences are fine. But if they are the basis of your faith, what happens when you have no experiences? God seems remote and distant and everything comes crashing down about your ears.
>
> The sand can be living to please yourself instead of living for God and giving to others.
>
> The sand can be always wanting to receive without giving first.
>
> And what does Jesus say about building on sand? He says only a foolish man does that, and when the storm comes the house crashes to the ground, 'and great was the fall of it'.
>
> During the early years of my Christian life I was taught that our reason was as important as the Bible. You came to the words of Scripture and applied your powers of reasoning to it. As a result, you only believed what you could rationally accept as true and were free to discard the rest.
>
> The outcome was a relatively powerless life and ministry.
>
> Then I began to see the Word with the eyes of the Spirit. I began to believe it instead of criticise it! I began to accept it, instead of pull it apart so that I needn't believe it.
>
> And the outcome was a new life and a new ministry in which I have seen the power of God at work in ways that I never thought possible, but in ways that GOD PROMISES IN HIS WORD.[21]

When the Word of God is believed, Colin teaches, what God

says can be translated into action, God's action in people's lives and in the world around them. Believing God in this way is not a 'mindless' process, rather it leads to minds through which God can reveal His wisdom, understanding and truth. This then imparts to the Christian a new way of thinking and perceiving, with situations now viewed from a divine as opposed to a human standpoint. It is all part of the renewal of our minds, or as Colin puts it pithily, 'a life-long retraining programme'.

Colin preaches that you cannot separate Jesus from His words; and that if a person accepts the authority of Jesus in his life, then he also accepts the authority of His words. But it is not a matter of slavish adherence or grudging obedience, because if Jesus is Lord, then His words are precious and life-giving, and a rich source of guidance and comfort.

Colin draws a distinction between those Christians who turn to the Bible only when they have a need and those who live by God's promises continually; only when the latter approach applies can they really be living by faith and trust. He constantly teaches that the promises of God need to be living words deep within a person: they may exist in a person's head whereas they need to be transferred to the heart. He suggests the following method for storing God's promises within the heart:

First: take one of the promises from either the Old or New Testament. As a covenant child of God you inherit them all!

Second: sit down quietly in a reasonably comfortable chair and be as relaxed as possible. Spend a few moments letting the tensions of the day flow out of your body and mind. Deliberately allow your muscles to slacken.

Third: take a minute or two handing over to God the things that are of concern to you, so that these will not get in the way of hearing and receiving what God is saying in His Word. This is *not* a time to sit down and think about your problems. Just let go of them for a few minutes. You may need to ask

God to forgive you and you may need to forgive someone who has wronged or hurt you.

Fourth: take the promise that you have decided to use and repeat it slowly to yourself a number of times. If you are on your own, you may like to speak it aloud, but quietly. This often helps concentration. Don't try to work out the meaning of the words in your mind. 'Hear' God speak them to you, to your spirit. Repeat the promise over and over again. 'Receive' it. At first, you will only be able to spend a couple of minutes with the one sentence. As you become used to this method of prayer, you will be able to concentrate on the same sentence for a much longer period of time. It is better to spend a few minutes, two or three times a day, than trying to 'receive' for too long at any one time.

Nothing dramatic is going to happen. Often you may feel that nothing at all has happened. But as you persist with the same word of promise for a week or more, it becomes part of you, and of your inheritance as a child of your heavenly Father.[22]

Colin Urquhart does not view Scripture as one might view a textbook on an academic subject which we are invited to analyse and even disagree with. He sees it as God's dynamic Word which speaks personally to individual people who, when they learn to receive the words for themselves, find God's Word becoming an indispensable part of their thinking. This then leads to action that is controlled and guided by God's Word.

Revival

Colin Urquhart is deeply interested in the history of revival world-wide. More importantly perhaps, he has experienced local revivals on at least three occasions: at St Hugh's, The Hyde and, more recently, at Roffey Place. In his preaching he constantly affirms that revival is coming nationally, a refrain that some of his close associates occasionally find tedious. This doesn't deter him, and he continues to proclaim his belief that a dynamic sweep of the Holy Spirit in revival power is coming to this country.

Revival, classically defined, has to do with a mighty out-pouring of God's Spirit. It is a miraculous occurrence that cannot be manipulated (as often happens in evangelism) or artificially manufactured because it is a sovereign act of God. All revivals to a lesser or greater extent are a return to Pentecost, with clear demonstrations of the Holy Spirit's power. Being 'heaven-sent', revivals do not spring out of the normal activities of the Christian church, which, in part at least, explains their freshness and vigour. One modern Christian leader, Selwyn Hughes, has described revival in terms of 'times of refreshing', when there is an extraordinary sense of God's pristine holiness, new insights into Jesus's work on the cross, an intense interest in prayer and Bible reading, and a feeling of extraordinary fervour and excitement amongst Christians.

Colin defines revival in terms of a bringing back to life of the life of God in a nation. He believes that only revival can transform a country at all levels: economic, political, social and religious. He believes with equal tenacity that it is God's will to extend His kingdom in Britain, when God's will will clearly be done on earth as it is in heaven.

Colin believes that revival starts with Christians. Their primary motive for deserving revival must be for the glory of God. Christians should care deeply that God is not being glorified in our nation, with its moral laxity, nor in His church when that church is characterised by unbelief, compromise, traditionalism and torpor. By the same token, God is not being glorified in the life of the individual believer when he/she is not enjoying the fullness of the life that Jesus promised, 'unless rivers of living water are flowing from his innermost being, unless everything in his life is of faith.'

God's agent for revival is the Holy Spirit, but there can be no limitation imposed on His work. In fact, there is only one kind of revival: a Holy Spirit revival. Colin finds it is necessary to stress this because there are people who want revival confined and restricted to their particular denomination or grouping. 'All such distinctions,' says Colin, 'are irrelevant in a time of revival. God's people become hungry for God Himself; they recognise their need for more of Him'. When this happens they are 'more open to Him, more able to receive from Him, more determined to live in a way that glorifies Him.' At a time of revival, too, the Holy Spirit reveals Jesus as the one who is to be sovereign in every area of life.

In his preaching and teaching, Colin refers to two primary types of revival: personal and corporate.

Personal revival

Personal revival begins with an appreciation of what God has done for each individual believer.

Believers all need revival continuously, and from time to time, they need to check their lives against the teaching of the Bible. Colin suggests the following check-list to evaluate how fully (or otherwise) the individual person is living the life God has made available to us:

1 Your life as a child of God – Do you still question God's love for you or His acceptance of you? Your relationship with other children of God – Do you love them as Christ has loved you?

2 Your life as a son of God – Are you living by faith in what God says you are able to do, exercising authority over temptation, sin and the powers of darkness? Do you submit to the authority of your heavenly Father as Jesus did?

3 Do you keep looking back over your past? Do you still

consider yourself a victim of your past? Are you holding on to hurt, bitterness or resentment instead of believing that the old has passed away and the new has come? Do you speak of yourself or others in a belittling way as if you still belong to the world and not to Jesus?

4   You are called to be holy. Is there secret sin in your life? Do you cherish any unholy desires? Do you give your mind over to ungodliness by dwelling on unholy things or allowing yourself to be influenced by reading or watching things that are ungodly? Do you allow yourself to come under the influence of wordly attitudes through relationships with others?

5   As one who lives in Christ, do you speak of yourself and of what you can do with genuine faith? Do you still try to control your own life or do you allow Jesus to do so? Are you trying to hold on to your own identity apart from Christ? Do your allow Him to be Lord of every area of your life?

6   Are you yielded to the life of the Holy Spirit, so you can be led by the Spirit as a son of God? Do you try to limit or control the working of the Holy Spirit in your life in any way? Do you earnestly desire the gifts of the Holy Spirit? Do you freely express the life of the Spirit? In what ways does your self-life restrict the development of the fruit of love, joy, peace, patience, kindness, goodness, faithfulness, gentleness and self-control?

7   Do you grumble, complain and moan about your circumstances? Are you faithful in your giving that you may live in God's abundance? Are you negative in your attitudes instead of being gracious, generous and positive in the way you act and react?

8   Instead of walking in victory, do you live in fear, failure and defeat? Do you believe your problem rather than the answer of the problem? Do you listen to feelings, reason and circumstances rather than what God says to you through His Word?

9   Do you spend sufficient time in prayer, in seeking God, in study of His Word, in listening to His voice? Do you make excuses for your prayerlessness and lack of spiritual vitality, claiming that you are too busy with other things to give God His rightful place?

10 In what other ways does self get in God's way in your life? What areas of your personality and character do not reveal Jesus and deny your life in Him? Are you selfish, jealous, angry? Do you shut yourself off from other people instead of being one who reveals Jesus to others? Are you too concerned with self to want your life to be used by God to love and serve others in the Church and the world? Are you lax in your spiritual discipline? Is there any lack of integrity?[23]

This, in his view, is the first step towards personal revival, a fuller realisation of God's kingdom life within a person. It begins with repentance, and continues by believing and acting upon the good news of what God has done for each individual person. Only as individuals come into a place of personal revival can a fellowship, church or nation be revived and live, in a real sense, to God's glory.

Corporate revival

That the church needs a corporate revival is self-evident in Britain today. Revival starts, Colin teaches, with a return to faith in God's Word, 'not merely assent that this is the revealed word of truth, but a *living faith*' which causes Christians to live out the Word in their daily lives, thus influencing their families, work-places and churches in radical ways. But faith without love is empty, and God's purpose is that faith will work through love: there has to be a revival of love, a genuine commitment to each other, living for others instead of ourselves in a selfish way. Thus there needs to be a corporate repentance for such things as criticism and judgement of each other, party spirit, jealousy, selfish ambition and worldly pride; a corporate repentance, too, of any church activity that is of the flesh and not of the Spirit. Self-centredness, tepid love, the attitude that says 'it's our church and not God's', lack of compassion for the poor and needy – all such attitudes, which are a negation of the gospel of Christ, must be repented of before God can bless His body with revival. Indeed:

> Revival can only come to a congregation when the people there realise that they are part of the Church for the glory of God and the fulfilment of His purposes, not for any selfish motives of their own. The Church does not exist for itself, nor for its members, but for the glory of God, to be His instrument in the world. Believers are to express His life in every area of society.[24]

The fruit of revival among believers is a spiritual awakening in the nation as a whole, whose features Colin highlights as follows:

> Multitudes of People turn to Christ and are brought into the Kingdom. Because of the holiness in which God's people are living, the convicting power of the Holy Spirit works much more freely. Many who have been resistant to the gospel become aware of their sinful state and need of God.

> A national revival that lasts a considerable length of time causes moral and social principles of that society to be changed. Godly ideals are restored to the nation. There is a much greater God-consciousness. There is also an intensification in the conflict between light and darkness, good and evil, faith and unbelief. But undoubtedly, in-roads are made by the gospel into areas of sin and depravity, leading to a reduction in crime, vice and other ungodly pursuits. The Church permeates as effective leaven in the lump of the world.[25]

143

Holiness

The emphasis on holiness in Colin's preaching is closely related to the theme of revival.

Colin sees holiness as something utterly positive. It is to be like Jesus, to live as He lived. He puts it neatly: 'To live a holy life, the Christian needs to be full of Jesus, full to overflowing with His love, life, joy and power.' In other words, to reflect Jesus in our everyday attitudes and actions which, inevitably, involves a deliberate turning away from sin in all its various forms. The metaphor he often uses is that of 'holy fire' which refines and purges, where necessary, the dross in a Christian's life: it is, of course, the holy fire of God's Spirit.

The secret of holiness, as Colin preaches it, is to be concerned with God's holiness:

> Holiness happens in our lives, not through a strenuous sifting out of sin, not by any self-awareness or introspective processes, but by looking away from ourselves to the One who is Himself holy, the One who has created us to be like Him. It is He who will point out the blemishes and create in us a desire to be rid of them. 'Blessed is the man whose sin the Lord does not count against him and in whose spirit is found no deceit.' (Ps. 32:2)

> We only become like the one we look at. To look in upon ourselves will result in a constant sense of unworthiness and failure. With our eyes on Him, seeing who He is in His holiness, we shall grow into His likeness.[26]

Thus, as the individual Christian is renewed from one degree of glory to another, he will find himself with a new spirit of sensitivity to God, with greater desires for purity of heart, a daily dying to sin and self and a movement away from everything that displeases God, a sharper sense of brokenness before God (see Psalm 51), with an overwhelming compassion for non-Christians, a heightened desire to keep his mind free of Satan's activity (see Ephesians 6:16), and with an increased generosity in giving to other people, be that in time or money or merely helpful advice.

It follows that when a sufficient number of individual believers begin to live like this, the church as a whole will begin to be affected in its daily life, exhibiting wholeness, which is a basic meaning of holiness, evangelism and worship. It will, in turn, become the spearhead of revival and thus begin to affect the life of the nation.

Ultimately Colin's preaching on the whole concept of holiness may be distilled down to what he calls 'the basic question', the question of control in our lives: God's or ours.[27] All too often when Christians are confronted with something they don't want to do, a debate rages within them as to whether they will be obedient or not. Such a situation, Colin teaches, is serious, 'for what is ultimately at stake is the whole matter of God's authority in their lives, whether Jesus is allowed to exercise His Lordship over them'. This means that we are called to follow Jesus unconditionally, a commitment that ought to be made, Colin believes, at the very beginning of our Christian experience:

> Sadly that does not always happen because of the way the Gospel is presented. People are often invited to come to Christ because of the benefits they will receive as a result. Those benefits certainly exist and are, in themselves, amazing; but they should not be the principal reason for giving ourselves to the Lord.
>
> We come to Him for His sake first, that His purpose might be worked out in us, that we might do His will, not our own. Until that principle is clearly established, we will constantly be preferring our own wills to His. The purpose He has for us will be hindered again and again by our disobedience.
>
> Because they have not yet faced this basic question of ownership, many ministers are unprepared to lead their people in obedience to God's Word and Spirit.[28]

The same commitment will apply equally to our time, resources, and money.

To sum up, Colin's preaching on the subject of holiness involves a number of key principles: holiness is God's great desire for the lives of Christians; because He is holy, we are expected to be holy also; holiness is to be 'full of Jesus' which cannot come about without the refining fire of the Holy Spirit in our lives each day; and holiness is not a burden of restrictions to be borne by believers, rather 'liberation from all burdens, freedom to celebrate God's abundant goodness and to joyfully sing of His righteousness'[29]; perhaps, above all, it is a positive quality that distinguishes the Christian from the non-Christian, faith in Jesus from mere religious observance.

Healing

A distinctive feature of charismatic renewal in the last thirty years has been its emphasis on healing. Michael Harper says: 'I have never seriously doubted that Jesus performed the miracles recorded in the Gospels. But it was not until 1962 that I began to see stories in the Gospels as encouraging us to expect the same healings today.'[30]

Despite the increased sense of expectancy that began to appear with the development of the charismatic movement, and has grown ever since, large sections of the church remain nervous about some of the approaches to healing, particularly the exaggerated claims made from time to time. This is a controversial area, therefore, and one in which Colin has played a leading part.

Colin does not preach healing as an end in itself rather, he expects powerful signs and wonders (including healing) to accompany the preaching of the Word of God. He does not present himself as a healer or miracle worker. But, armed with what he frequently calls 'the kingdom message', he looks to see his words confirmed by God 'with demonstrations of kingdom power'. This gospel of the kingdom embraces the whole counsel of God, and he preaches that signs and wonders are the evidence that kingdom power and authority are still given to men and women today. He outlines his perception of the relationship between the spoken word, faith and works in *The Positive Kingdom*:

> Signs are the evidence that Kingdom power and authority is still given to men. The first disciples did not manifest such gifts as perfectly as Jesus. Their perception, faith and authority fell far short of His. There was nothing imperfect in Jesus to hinder His unity with His Father. The works of heaven could be seen supremely in Him.

> Nevertheless, the disciples did see God working powerfully through them. The seventy-two were overjoyed that 'even the demons submit to us in your name.' (Luke 10:17)

> The disciples were sent out in Jesus's name and all the works they performed were in His name – on His behalf, with His power and authority.

> Similarly today, believers are not only to speak in His name but work in His name, on His behalf, with His power and authority. Anyone who has faith in Jesus will do what He did – and even greater things still.[31]

To Colin, kingdom life and kingdom power are inseparable, because as he often preaches, they were perfectly united in Jesus: 'As the early Christians lived the teaching He had given, so they saw God's powerful acts which demonstrated His kingly presence among them.'

Colin's views on healing are not acceptable to dispensationalists who view signs and wonders as obsolete today, relegating them to the pages of the New Testament only; to those who regard signs and wonders as the normal solution for every occurrence of sickness, corruption or sin in the life of the church; or to those who regard signs and wonders as a technique which if properly performed will enable the church to exhibit a dynamic power at the very least equal to that of the early church.

Opposition, however, does not deter him, and his preaching will always be accompanied by his willingness to pray for the healing of people spiritually, emotionally or physically. The reason for this is that God's healing power came to him as a revelation from God; and, as with other key areas of his life and ministry, once Colin receives something in this way, he acts upon it, putting it into practice.

Other emphases

Other recurrent emphases in Colin's preaching include the *kingdom of God*, which he portrays as unfailingly positive and in total contrast to the kingdom of darkness (Satan's dominion) where everything is negative: 'Just as the kingdom of God reflects the nature of the one who rules it, so does the kingdom of darkness.'[32] Colin also stresses that the kingdom of God is meant to be a practical reality in the daily lives of Christian men and women.

Another emphasis is *prayer*: as our fellowship with God is furthered through reading the Bible and prayer, these two activities are primary emphases in his preaching. Prayer, too, is an important part of Colin's preparation for preaching. Recently I accompanied Colin and his team to an afternoon and evening celebration on the south coast. Arriving at the church with only half an hour to spare before starting the meeting, the first thing he did was to engage in prayer and praise with his team. There was no feeling of rush or tension because each person realised that it was vitally important to hear from God. Then, in the evening, at least fifty minutes was spent in prayer, speaking in tongues, reading passages of Scripture before the celebration started. Clearly Colin is a man of prayer himself; prayer comes as naturally as breathing to him, and it is as vital, too. His book *Listen and Live* is the product of a life devoted to prayer and listening to God.

Love: is another emphasis of his preaching. 'We love', says the Word of God, 'because he first loved us' (1 John 4:19). It is a truth that needs to become a personal revelation for each Christian, then shared and communicated to others. It is not a sentimental or gushing thing, but a dedicated commitment to each other, always desiring the best for the other person, even (perhaps especially) if hurt has been caused.

The person of Christ, another prominent theme, is closely related, both in the New Testament and in Colin's preaching, to that of love, which binds all the other emphases together in his ministry. As Colin says,

> God, in His love, had to send His own Son to die on the cross. That was the cost He had to pay to enable men to be forgiven, and to break the power of sin in their lives; to enable them to be restored to fellowship with Himself, become members of His heavenly Kingdom and be restored to His divine glory.[33]

The *supremacy of Christ* is another related and dominant refrain, too:

> Jesus was the first to be raised from the dead. All those who belong to Him shall be raised with Him. He is the Lord who will always have supremacy, and when He returns everyone and everything that does not acknowledge His authority will pass away. In the new heaven and the new earth that God promises, He will reign without opposition from any spiritual or mortal beings.[34]

Some reflections

Colin Urquhart's preaching is biblical: his starting-point is that nothing is as important as the Scriptures of Truth. So he seeks to expound the Word of God and not merely to express his own ideas. He isn't concerned with what's topical at the moment, which means that his sermons have a timeless quality about them. They are also direct. He aims for an immediate impact on his congregation in terms of a faith-response, and he always emphasises the need for Christians to behave in a manner befitting the gospel of Christ.

What, then, explains the authority of Colin's preaching? An answer may be found by understanding his own attitude and desires: he wants divine authority to be pre-eminent in his preaching, not the transience of human wisdom. He wants God to speak, to influence the hearts, minds and emotions of his hearers. His sermons are designed to bring non-Christians to faith in Jesus Christ, and those who are already Christians to fruitfulness and maturity. In essence, Colin's sermons are the words God has revealed to him; and they are the passionate outflow of a man who has met with and encountered the living God.

Many years ago Dr Lloyd-Jones said that he could forgive the preacher almost anything provided he gave him 'a sense of God . . . if he gives me some dim glimpse of the majesty and glory of God, the love of Christ my Saviour, and the magnificence of the Gospel.'[35] A 'sense of God' is apparent whenever Colin preaches. It informs his writing, too, which is the subject of the next chapter.

THE AUTHOR

'Colin Urquhart has the ability to get through to ordinary readers in a way that few Christian authors can match,' says the renowned evangelist Michael Green, himself the author of many successful books. That Colin's books have, almost without exception, sold in many tens of thousands is a phenomenon of twentieth-century Christian publishing. Their marketing success is surprising, even astounding, to many people: the prose is simple and ordinary, the material is overwhelmingly biblical, with copious quotations from the Bible, while the subject-matter is serious – the work of the Holy Spirit, prayer, holiness. The format of some of them is disarmingly simple, but they obviously meet people's needs in ways that more intellectual, theologically sophisticated, more fluently written books do not. What explains the enormous success of Colin's books? Before answering this question we shall refer to each book in turn in an attempt to identify its main thrust and essence.

When the Spirit Comes (1974)

When the Spirit Comes has achieved cult status, and it is obligatory reading for all who wish to know something about charismatic renewal in the early nineteen seventies. Colin wrote it at the request of Edward England of Hodder & Stoughton and it placed St Hugh's, Lewsey at the heart of Anglican renewal. It also brought Colin to the attention of a much wider audience, both at home and abroad.

The theme of transformation dominates this book, first, that of Colin himself. Self-confessedly diffident, his ministry changed beyond recognition in Luton. At the outset of his time there he felt unable to lead his parishioners into a personal relationship with God. In fact, when he went there after serving in two other parishes the cry of his heart was: 'Lord we can't go on like this.' By the expression 'like this' he meant in a way unenlightened by the power of the Holy Spirit. But as time went on God showed him that he *could* minister in the Spirit's dynamic because he was a son of God. That startling realisation produced the change in his life and work, and *When the Spirit Comes* records how St Hugh's became internationally known as a centre for renewal and, later, revival. God's power was creatively at work within Colin, the curious fact being that he discovered the gifts of the Spirit long before he had heard of the charismatic movement. This is an important point because it shows that God through His Word was Colin's teacher and counsellor, not the pressure exerted by a movement. He could make mistakes free of the cloying effect that group expectations sometimes creates. From those days in Luton Colin has gone from strength to strength in terms of his own ministry and the effect it has on other people. Luton was not a pinnacle in his ministry; it was the start of a remarkable ministry that continues vibrantly today.

Second, the book deals with the transformation of the church itself. St Hugh's became a powerhouse for revival, attracting men and women from across the religious spectrum. As the Word of Gospel was applied at a living level, people came to see that the words of the Bible were words of truth about them personally and individually. They learned that they could live as 'new creatures' in Christ (2 Corinthians 5:17), but only as the Word of God became an indispensable part of them, personally and individually. They came to perceive that if the gospel is faithfully preached, they could expect to see God confirming the word with signs and wonders following. Anything less, Colin taught them, was an incomplete gospel, a veritable denial of the Word of God. So it was that an Anglican church in the Catholic tradition came alive in the Holy Spirit: 'The result was that people wanted Jesus', and were prepared to accept each other wherever they stood in relation to the renewal going on in the church at large. Colin writes:

> We were given a vision of all the members of our family standing in circles within the church building. There were circles of commitment. Some would choose to stand in the outermost circle on the fringe of things, others in the innermost circle sharing a common life together; others would choose one of the intermediary circles. We were shown that it is of importance that everybody should feel free to stand in the circle of their own choice, and also be free to move from one circle to another.

While it is not possible for there to be unanimity about what went on at St Hugh's (and the Synod's commissioned report highlighted that fact), it is interesting to record that Colin insisted that those 'older' members who found renewal rather difficult were free to attend the 8 a.m. communion service each Sunday, and a prayer group was reserved for them throughout his time in Luton.

When the Spirit Comes is a thrilling book, a voyage of discovery. It is simply and honestly written; the complexities and difficulties and failures are featured as well as the successes. Anyone can read it, as one reviewer said, 'without having to worry about religious terms'. It was and continues to be a success for one overriding reason: its central character is God. He is the hero of the story as, indeed, He is in all of Colin's books.

My Father is the Gardener (1977)

The genesis of Colin's second book may be traced to Luton, in fact he had hoped to complete it before leaving St Hugh's. This proved impossible. It began as a commentary on John 15:1–17 but was subsequently re-written, this time giving the essential teaching 'through fictitious characters in a fictitious setting'. Colin did not, however, intend the book to be read as a novel, rather as a teaching book in a 'readable and receivable style'. He gives an explanation of this in *Faith For the Future*:

> I know from personal experience how difficult it is to read 'heavy' books. Many people put them to one side and do not persevere with them. It is always my purpose to be simple and direct when either speaking or writing. If God is going to speak to ordinary folks like myself, He is going to use direct and easily understood methods.
>
> *My Father is the Gardener* is about the personal and corporate problems that need to be faced if churches are to be renewed in the Holy Spirit. People often ask if the characters are based on real individuals. They are not, but the characters and the situations that face them are all based on experience of people and how they relate. Readers often see themselves in one or more of th characters and that is the intention. For the book is not about living individuals, but people, and the problems they have as they face the Lord's purposes in their lives.[1]

As the publishers explained, 'the author uses fiction to examine the inner feelings and motives of his characters in a way that would not be possible in writing about living characters.' This mix of teaching (though not quite) and biography (though again not quite), linked by a fictional narrative, works, but only just.

The characters in *My Father is the Gardener* are all Anglican (very), British (very), and, above all, credible. Tom Billings, a busy thirty-five-year-old executive, father of two children, attends church routinely with the rest of the family because it adds 'solidity to their lives and a small measure of comfort to the rector'. The same lack of intimacy characterises the relationship between Tom and his wife Ann. He feels frustrated, not knowing what to believe; moreover the Bible has never been more than historic literature to him, certainly not a book capable of speaking to him personally. Yet feelings of futility torment him sufficiently to turn to the Bible.

Christopher Dean, the rector, has too much to do, and is haunted by the evident lack of power in his Christian life. As he explains to Tom and Ann:

> 'Time and time again, I have come to this point in my ministry,' he began. 'This is one time too many. You see, when I read the Bible, I come across so many things that we are told to do. I often want to do them, but I can't. I can't, because I haven't the power to do them. Jesus told His disciples to heal the sick and they did. They healed because He healed. I have never healed. For years I have seen sick people in their homes, in hospital; sometimes they are critically ill and are dying. I can do nothing for them except try to comfort them. I suppose I have become quite good at that, but it never satisfies me. When I go to see your boy, I shall see him lying there and I shall think, "Poor little mite." My prayer would be, "God, what a mess!" You see, Tom, I have reached a point of despair when it comes to sickness.'[2]

A pillar of respectability destined for 'higher things', Christopher seldom talks about his personal relationship with God. His wife Molly simply wants to be a 'normal sensible Christian' and shrinks away from any mention of the Holy Spirit.

The characters, then, are varied. Tom epitomises professional success, but has a sense of aimlessness aggravated by a superficial, hesitant faith. Christopher, well-liked by his congregation, is crippled by feelings of failure, while Molly, his wife, finds the whole concept of 'living in Jesus' alien and strange.

Claude Winter, the blustering egoist, is the parish politician who wants to dominate people and manipulates the decisions made at St Gabriel's, and he is feared by Christopher.

Each person, in different ways, experiences the renewal of God's Holy Spirit, in Claude's case as a result of sudden and dramatic illness; and Christopher's vision for St Gabriel's is clearly reminiscent of St Hugh's: a group of people brought alive in the Spirit, deeply committed to God and to each other in loving, caring relationships.

My Father is the Gardener has obvious technical weaknesses, such as the 'preachy-ness' of the opening sections which look like sermons placed in the mouth of a fictitious character; and the distinct feeling that everything is likely to end happily in the end, as it does. The strategy of linking plot and character via John chapter 15 caused one reviewer to comment: 'Regarded as a novel, the book is too contrived to be convincing.'

On the other hand, the book has equally distinctive positive qualities. The actions of the characters grow out of the people they are, for example. It graphically illustrates the joys and tensions of a church undergoing renewal and revival: the chapter describing Claude Winter's spiritual pilgrimage will strike a chord in the hearts of many people, as it did in mine. The conversations between the characters, too, are realistic. An apt example of this is the conversation between Ann Billings (whose life has been transformed by the Holy Spirit) and Molly, the rector's wife, who is reluctant to accept God's love:

'Why should that be such a problem? Don't you want to know Him?'

'I didn't at first. I would have been quite happy for our lives to have continued as they were before. Christopher and I have had a good life together. Then he changed. I must admit that I now see many qualities that I hadn't noticed in him before. Still, the change has threatened our life together. He has changed and I haven't. I was resentful at first. I wanted him to be the way I had always known him. Our holiday made me aware of the futility of that wish. I realised that I would have to join him if we were truly to be together again.' Molly stopped. Why was she saying all this to a comparative stranger?

'And so . . .' prompted Ann.

'Oh, I don't suppose you're really interested in my problems. Let me make you a cup of tea.'

'No,' said Ann firmly. 'Making cups of tea won't help, will it?'

Molly sighed. She felt trapped. Dare she confide in anyone her true problem?

'You don't believe He wants you, do you?'

Molly looked up sharply. 'Who do you mean?'

Ann smiled. 'I mean God, not Christopher.'

'How do you know that? I haven't told anyone, not even my husband.'

'Let's call it feminine intuition,' suggested Ann.

'That's not intuition, and you know it,' challenged Molly.

'What does it matter? Is it true?'

'Yes, it's true.'

'Why do you think that?'

'I've tried this business of placing my life in God's hands and nothing has happened. Absolutely nothing. In fact the very reverse. Any peace I ever had with God seems to have completely disappeared.'

Ann felt she was getting out of her depth. Christopher wouldn't be home for some time, as he was taking the Sunday School service. She shot a quick prayer heavenwards asking for inspiration.

'He does love you, Molly.'

'How do I know that? He has done nothing to prove His

love to me. The only person who has ever done that is Christopher.'[3]

Colin attempted something ambitious in *My Father is the Gardener*. It is much more than an exposition of charismatic experience in story form. Undoubtedly, at times the succession of supernatural events without sufficient background of the mundane and the ordinary makes the story seem unreal.

Edward England, however, provides an interesting insight into its success and influence: 'When Colin decided to write a novel I did not encourage him and had real problems when I read *My Father is the Gardener*. He was obviously a better preacher than novelist. Our relationship was so good that I told him so. He believed, however, he had been guided by the Holy Spirit to write the book as it would reach those who might not read his other publications. Rather than risk losing him we published. The book has been reprinted many times and some, including a close relative of Colin's, have made a commitment to Christ through reading it.'

Anything You Ask (1978)

This book explores the relationship between faith and prayer. Colin begins with this premise:

> Jesus told His disciples: 'If you ask anything in my name, I will do it' (John 14:14). If you ask ANYTHING!
>
> And the promise He gives: 'I WILL do it.' Not, 'I may do it', or 'I might', or 'I can', or 'I could'. 'I WILL DO IT.'
>
> At first sight those words seem so far from reality, as to be unbelievable. Yet Jesus said them and many like them, teaching that God wants to give you 'ANYTHING YOU ASK'.
>
> When I ask church-going people if they pray, most say that

they do. But if I go on to enquire if God does whatever they ask of Him there is usually an embarrassed silence or even laughter at the very suggestion. People seem to be saying: 'Oh we pray, but fancy expecting God to do everything we ask!'

And yet that is precisely what Jesus promises. Many of the things He says about prayer demonstrate that He knows His Father to be a generous Giver, One who loves His children so dearly that He *wants* to give to them.

This makes it even more remarkable that many Christians do not appear to believe that He is willing to give them whatever they ask. Some seem more concerned with discovering reasons why God should not give to them and meet their needs. Reasons or excuses.

Jesus wants us to be an asking people. And when we pray He wants us to know that we can expect to receive *whatever* we ask.[4]

Ultimately, for Colin, it is faith in Jesus's words that matters:

When your life is built securely on faith in the words of Jesus, it does not matter what storm breaks, what difficulties you are confronted with or how desperate things become. For you will see Him bringing you through to peace, joy and victory over all such oppressive circumstances. You will know that the One to whom we pray is the God who is faithful. 'I will not fail you or forsake you' (Josh. 1:5).[5]

Convinced that Jesus means what he says, Colin is prepared to take His promises literally, as he shows time and again throughout this book, notably in chapter 17, 'The Prayer of Faith'. In the context of healing, though, he is careful to indicate that the 'anything you ask' principle does not always mean instant answers to our prayers:

We pray according to the promises of Jesus. He does *not* promise instant answers to all our prayers. He does say:

'It will be done for you.' 'It will be given you.' 'It will be yours.' *It will be*.

Sometimes there will be instant healing; at other times a measure of improvement will be seen immediately in the patient. In some, there will be no discernible improvement in the condition, at the time. This is when it is so easy to believe your doubts, rather than the promises of Jesus. 'Nothing has happened.' 'It hasn't worked.' 'God doesn't want to heal me.'

'Believe that you have received it, and it will be yours,' Jesus says. Go on believing until you see the answer, the promise fulfilled. Don't give up! Or be tempted to believe your doubts. Don't be concerned if you have not experienced or felt anything.

Why was nearly everyone who came to Jesus healed instantly, and yet that is obviously not the case at healing services today?

At healing services Jesus is ministering His healing power, but imperfect channels, with imperfect faith, exercise less than the total authority of Jesus. Obviously, there are some who come looking to the man ministering and not to the Lord: so that can lead to disappointment. There will be others who are hoping for the best, and who do not believe that they have received what they asked for. There are others who come wanting only to receive and not to give to the Lord; they are not seeking first the kingdom of God.[6]

Nor can we isolate our prayers from the rest of life:

Their fruitfulness will depend largely upon the kind of life you are living; whether you live to give to God, or whether you are still living for yourself, 'choked by cares and riches and pleasures of life'. Whether you only want to receive, or become a generous giver.

It is not only worldliness that 'chokes' the seed; Jesus says it is also choked by 'cares'. By problems, worries, anxiety, fear. All these things are the opposite of faith.

160

And some fell into good soil and grew, and yielded a hundredfold (Luke 8:8). And as for that in the good soil, they are those who, hearing the word, hold it fast in an honest and good heart, and bring forth fruit with patience (Luke 8:15).

The fruitful hearers are the believers. They not only hear the word; they *hold it fast*, no matter what the situation, no matter how many doubts are pushed in their direction. They hold on to the promise of God. They believe Him.

Their believing comes from the heart. And they *bring forth fruit with patience*. They wait for the fulfilment of the promises of God, knowing that He will be faithful.[7]

Anything You Ask is a practical book. It teaches how to claim God's promises and how to pray the prayer of faith. Some Christians may balk at the audacity of Jesus's promises; Colin simply believes them and invites his readers to do the same. This is, I believe, the source of the book's power, as the *Church of England Newspaper* reviewer recognised: 'The publishers claim that its thirty-three chapters "can revolutionise your life" is for once not an exaggeration. If you have been vague or apologetic about prayer, it will change your tune.'

In Christ Jesus (1981)

In Christ Jesus is designed for 'defeated' Christians and attempts to answer this question: 'Is it possible to know victory over temptation, weakness, futility and spiritual inadequacy?' Colin answers the questions by looking at what God has done for the believers in Jesus, the believer's new life in Jesus, and how to live in Jesus.

The crux of the argument is found in chapter 11, where Colin writes:

The old sinful nature has been crucified. That is a fact, but we can still live in ignorance or unbelief of that fact and imagine that we are still bound by sin . . .

If we deny that we are in Christ, we not only argue with the teaching of the Scripture, we also render ourselves ineffective in combating sin. It is because we are in Him that we can be built up in His life and His truth, and so be set free from the desire to please ourselves and oppose Him.

It will be important for us to build up a picture from the Scriptures of what it means to live 'in Christ Jesus'. For only then shall we see ourselves as God sees us. He does not see us separated from Him but as living in Him . . .

Once we know and reckon ourselves to be dead in Christ, then the way is clear for us to be built up in our understanding of the new nature that God has given us, the truths that apply to us as those who live in Him, and the power that He makes available to us.

To live in the revelation that you are a new creature living in Christ, and no longer bound by the old, sinful nature, will enable you to die daily to sin.[8]

Spiritual growth comes, in Colin's view, from learning to trust the facts of what God has done for each person in Jesus, from seeing ourselves as he sees us ('in Jesus', alive in Him and victorious in the power of the Holy Spirit), not as the world or Satan would see us.

This is a substantial book on the vital topic of the 'life in grace'. It is, in fact, a handbook of scriptural truths designed by Colin for daily meditation, and is not meant to be read straight through. It is not easy reading. It was, however, warmly received by a number of discerning reviewers. Michael Green, for example, referred to the overall impact of *In Christ Jesus* as being 'helpful and constructive, even if at times it is over-simplistic'. He also said this: 'It will teach believers to look *up* to the Lord and his provision, not *in* to their doubts and fears and sins . . . The book has a direct approach to the reader, with no references to the works of others, only a great exposure to the text of Scripture . . . It is calculated to stir up in the believer the faith that can claim great things from God.'

Another prominent Anglican, Michael Baughen, described the book as a *tour de force* and as a 'rich feasting on the Word of God'. He then commented:

> Overall the book is a magnificent piece of work. It covers carefully the Cross, eternal life, being dead and raised, and similar aspects involved in understanding the depth of being in Christ. There is a most welcome insistence on trusting the facts rather than the feelings and on appropriating what is ours in Christ rather than seeking a further blessing.

Michael Baughen concluded his review,

> There are many helpful examples in the book but usually from his counselling and thus lacking something of the cut and thrust of living in Christ Jesus in the midst of the everyday life of this fallen world.

> This is a glorious exposition of life in Christ Jesus which deeply grasps Scripture with helpful discernment. It is a book that is far from being a charismatic-labelled book even if it has occasional trips in that direction.

> The overall effect is to feel one's soul enriched and to want to live more fully in Christ Jesus. The book draws us to Christ and in that light other matters are secondary.

The reviewers were united in stressing the book's accessibility; its helpful advice, both for younger and older Christians, to approach the Christian life positively in the light of the Bible; its insistence that the Christian life is meant to be a continual experience of God at work in us: our experience raised to the level of His Word; its illustrations which are drawn from Colin's pastoral experience; and its faith-building qualities. 'The book will help many', wrote one reviewer, 'to trust more, obey more and rejoice more, and therefore must be welcomed.' Here, then, is relevant, thought-provoking teaching on fundamental aspects of a Christian's growth 'in Jesus', all lavishly illustrated from the Bible, with sound advice and practical guidelines for mature Christian living.

Faith For The Future (1982)

Faith For The Future is the sequel to *When the Spirit Comes*. It charts Colin's life and ministry from the time he left St Hugh's at the end of 1975 to the early nineteen eighties. This volume offers valuable insights into Colin's ministry. These include his daily practice of listening to God; the confidence he felt as he fulfilled the Lord's commission to preach the gospel, make disciples, heal the sick, and give generously to others; the continuing need to live by faith and in the power of the Holy Spirit; the commitment to the ministry of healing; the constant discipline of discipleship; the emphasis on revival; and his leadership of the Bethany Fellowship.

The book also tells the continuing story of renewal, healing and evangelism that came world-wide through Colin's preaching. During these years many lives were transformed. In Alberta, a man collapsed with a stopped heart, having previously suffered a heart attack, but, after prayer, he revived and doctors could find no trace of even the heart attack. In Brisbane, Australia, a victim of polio for twenty years left his crutches behind. Even more startling, in South Africa the words of the blind man Jesus encountered are echoed: 'When I came to the meeting I was blind, and now I can see.' The book is a powerful challenge to faith. Colin writes:

> God wants to give us all faith for the future, to believe that He will move among us in the coming years with greater power. He wants to give us His faith and teach us to see things as He sees them. He wants to bring us to the end of compromise in our lives and ministries. He calls all who belong to Him to be part of His building work as He fulfils

His promise to build His Church. He wants our confidence to
be in Him as we fulfil His commission to proclaim the gospel
of the Kingdom of God, to make disciples, to heal the sick
and give freely to others as He has given to us. He calls us
to share His concern for the lost, to participate in the cost of
intercession, to break the hold the powers of darkness have
over many who reject the Saviour.[9]

It is a challenge accompanied by confidence because Jesus is
'the author and perfector of our faith'.

Faith For The Future is a great encouragement to the
faith of individual believers. As Jim Graham said in his
review for *Renewal*, 'we are left with the impression that you
are not looking backward, nor indeed inward, but outward
and onward.' It was an enormous publishing success and
was nominated 'Hodder Christian Paperback of the Year'.
Some reviewers, like Michael Green, expressed surprise at
the accolade, for the following reasons: 'It is yet another of
the "inspirational" books, full of miracles and the personal
pronoun. It is prone to exaggeration. A glowing picture emerges
of the community at The Hyde, but its problems receive less
attention. [Urquhart] says that he asks those who have been
healed at his meetings to stand and indicate: this is not always
the case, and sometimes there is little evidence afterwards to
substantiate the claims . . . The book is short on teaching and
betrays even more clearly the triumphalism that can occur
when good and godly men write about their own ministry.'

Some of Michael Green's comments are valid. There is,
for example, an imbalance in Colin's portrait of life at The
Hyde: there were strains and tensions which he does not
reflect. Green's observations, however, must not be allowed
to obscure the central aim of *Faith For The Future*: to record
a story of growth and the coming into being of a community
of helpers and fellow-workers at The Hyde and of personal
growth in faith and in commitment to Christ and the kingdom
of God.

Holy Fire (1984)

Holy Fire is strong meat. It preserves a fundamental emphasis in Colin's preaching and writing, that of revival. Before revival can come, there must be a resurgence of holiness (defined as 'being like Jesus'). First, personally in terms of humility, meekness, righteousness, mercy, purity of heart, peacefulness, faithful love and generous giving; second, corporately through a holy church; and third, prophetically, through worship.

Holy Fire is an impassioned plea that holiness and the life of the Spirit should be closely linked together. It is a most welcome antidote to the oft-expressed emphasis in charismatic circles that to speak in tongues and to perform miracles of healing is all that is necessary to glorify God. This volume belongs to the 'middle ground' of solid scriptural exegesis, and is a valuable corrective to the approach that the Spirit is entirely understood through experience.

The Positive Kingdom (1985)

(L1)*The Positive Kingdom* was written for 'all those who feel they have little or no hope', so that they may 'come to know the power of the Positive Kingdom in their lives'. Colin claims that many Christians have gained the impression that the kingdom can only be entered beyond death, and that there is always an element of uncertainty as to whether they will be accepted by God. This is not what the New Testament teaches, which in Colin's opinion means that many Christians either labour under a misapprehension or are ignorant of what the Bible teaches, and the book attempts to redress this false notion.

The Positive Kingdom will cause such people to think again about the nature of God's kingdom which, he writes, reflects the nature of the King of heaven, and is absolutely positive. In this sense, of course, it is in total contrast to the negativity of Satan's kingdom: he wants to trap men and women, God wants to set them free. It was to liberate people that Jesus came, Colin stresses, and the glorious, eternal kingdom is meant to be a personal possession here and now; the enjoyment of eternal life begins amidst the realities of everyday life.

These themes are then illustrated – in Colin's usual thorough way – in terms of New Testament teaching, culminating in the concept of 'kingdom glory'. In this context he strikes the note of consummation:

> There is glory to come for all the children of the Kingdom, for their King will return to the earth in triumph. They are to prepare for that time, not knowing when it will be, but living as if it were to be today.

> Whenever there has been revival in the Church's history, there has been expectancy of Christ's return, accompanied by a sense of urgency in the preaching of the Kingdom. His return will be a glorious event for the saved, but will involve judgement for the lost. Renewed faith in the great hope that God's Kingdom will be established and recognised everywhere, brings with it the sense of urgency in reaching as many of the lost as possible with the truth, so that they may have opportunity to repent of their sins and be born again into the Kingdom of God.[10]

The Positive Kingdom is direct, straightforward teaching. It is a valuable resource for young Christians looking for a simply-written synopsis of fundamental aspects of the faith.

Receive Your Healing (1986)

Receive Your Healing is probably Colin's most controversial book. It is a comprehensive treatment of his views on healing as it operates today and as it has operated in his own healing ministry for over twenty-five years. At the risk of seeming simplistic, its message may be summed up in a series of axioms. First, healing is always God's best purpose for those who believe in Jesus Christ, to heal them. Second, sickness is a failure to live like Jesus. Third, it can never be God's perfect will for Christians to be sick. Fourth, healing is an integral part of evangelism, and the gospel proclaimed must also be the gospel demonstrated. Here he distinguishes sharply between suffering (for the sake of the gospel) and sickness. Fifth, failure to heal is either through lack of faith in the sick person or in the healer or in the church. Sixth, all the spiritual gifts are available to every believer.

The key statement for an understanding of Colin's views on healing is found early in this book: 'The matter is very simple. If God wants you to be healthy, and that is certainly His best purpose, then *it is right to look to Him with faith, and pray to be healed*.' His faith in God's healing power – and desire to do so – is total, and something of this faith is communicated when people read his books. Here is the testimony of a chronic alcoholic who read *Anything You Ask* and was healed of his addiction:

> In my darkest time I said the prayer you suggested in your book in desperation to Jesus. I'd never bothered with God at all very much and didn't really expect miracles . . . in desperation I prayed and God answered . . .

> Today life is lovely. I love being alive. I haven't drunk for fifteen months and can cope with life as good as any. Of course there are still day-to-day problems, but knowing I have God in control I don't get as anxious as before.[11]

A similar thing occurred – though this time a physical healing – when a forty-four-year-old woman with breast cancer read *Receive Your Healing*. She wrote:

> When I was diagnosed as having breast cancer – I have a

young family – I was shattered. When I asked some Christian
leaders to pray for me, I was told not to get 'hung up' on
healing because 'not everyone was healed'. Your book gave
me new hope and courage. I have prayed and the tumour is
shrinking.

Opinions regarding *Receive Your Healing* are deeply divided.
Some find it encouraging, uplifting and faith-building, because
here is a man who clearly takes the Bible seriously. Others
point to the fact that Colin appears to ignore those passages
of Scripture which contradict his overall argument. Yet a third
group of people find his premise that it can never be God's
will for a Christian to be sick questionable. The reviewer on
the *Church of England Newspaper*, for example, asserts that
'countless Christians down the ages have given themselves
unreservedly to the service of the kingdom, who have died
of plague and tragic accidents, meaning for them untimely
death. The case of David Watson is just one recent example',
and asks this question: 'Dare we suggest God's power and love
did not extend to such people? Surely not.' A fourth group
believe that miracles and healings are for today but that glory
through suffering is for today, too. Such people would plead
most strongly for a theology of suffering as well as a theology
of healing.

Listen and Live (1987)

Sub-titled 'Using the Bible in Prayer', *Listen and Live* is Colin's
attempt to answer two of the questions most frequently asked by
Christians: 'How can I pray more effectively?' and, 'How can I
receive from God the blessings He promises?' His response is
to offer a *way* of praying that has proved to be both effective
and powerful in his own life. His method consists of ten
sections: *opening sentence*: as it sets the theme, it should
be read slowly and thoughfully; *brief prayer*: asking God to

fill the time of prayer with His presence; *Scripture reading*: read aloud to aid concentration; *relaxation*: it is easier to concentrate when relaxed; 'come to me': giving to God the burdens or any besetting worries; *forgive others*: making sure no resentment or anger is stored up when others are forgiven; *meditation sentence*: repeating the Scripture sentence again, so that the Lord's Word enters the person's spirit; *prayer for others*: directing the words received personally towards other people; *praise*: thanking God for His love and presence in prayer; *closing prayer*: a prayer of consecration to God.

The essence of Colin's method is two-fold: first its power is derived from using the words of Jesus and other scriptures in prayer; and second it is effective because God 'will always honour His own words'.

There then follow seventy-eight prayer outlines. One of them, entitled 'The Truth about Yourself' (based on 2 Corinthians 5:17), reads as follows:

God's Word is truth; that is why it is so important to read His Word, to feed on it and to receive the Spirit, life and truth that are in His Word. Remember, agree with what He says about you and about all who are in Christ, even if you do not fully understand what the Scriptures mean. Affirm the truths for yourself.

Therefore there is now no condemnation for those who are in Christ Jesus (Rom. 8:1). I deserved to be condemned, but God by His loving grace has saved me. I do not have to allow the enemy to put me under any feelings of condemnation. God has put me into Christ – and there can be no condemnation in Him! I am not rejected by God; I am accepted by Him!

Christ is in me so my spirit is alive because of righteousness. I need no longer consider myself unrighteous because God has made me righteous in His sight. I have Christ as my righteousness because God has put me in Him.

I can walk not according to the flesh but according to the

Spirit. To set my mind on pleasing myself, to dwell on my feelings, doubts and fears is spiritual death. Harmony and fellowship with the Lord are not possible if what I believe and say is hostile to God's Word. To set my mind on the Spirit, who declares God's Word to me – that is life and peace.

Notice the way in which the truths of Scripture are personally appropriated. I see myself as God sees me and speak to myself as He speaks of me in His Word. These same truths are true for you. As you learn to be still and to receive from God His words will become part of your thinking and believing.

Hear the Spirit taking the truth of God's Word and declaring it to you now. You are a new creation. The old has gone in your life and the new *has* come. Hear Him and believe him.[12]

Inevitably reservations were expressed about Colin's method because many people believe that prayer should always be spontaneous. Others believe that the disciplined form of such a method is merely a cover for a legalistic approach to prayer. The most strident criticisms of *Listen and Live* were voiced in the *Church of England Newspaper*, which headed its review 'Spiritual fast food sampled'. Peter Akehurst commented, 'The teaching is direct though manipulative and highly experiential. Random words of Scripture are said to be God/Jesus saying this to you now, and are used to speak faith to oneself.' He also asks, 'In terms of the sub-title, is this really "using the Bible" or selecting special bits? And isn't "using the Bible" manipulative in the extreme and not quite what we aim at in prayer?' He concludes, '*Listen and Live* contains much helpful advice . . . but seems short as whole-food for the life of prayer.'

A balanced perspective on *Listen and Live* – which Colin intends as a *way* of praying – must, however, give due place to a number of other features. The method is adaptable (the prayer time can be as long or as short as the person requires), while the words of Scripture can become a part of a person's thinking and inner life, as countless letters to Colin bear witness. It also provides a framework for a vital activity in the life of faith, and it allows for teaching to be imbibed without the same need for concentration as, say, in listening to a sermon.

Personal Victory (1988)

Victorious Christian living is a perennial theme in Colin's writing and preaching. *Personal Victory* is based on the premise that Jesus does not promise His followers an easy life, neither does he offer trite answers to the complexity of people's needs. 'Instead', says Colin, 'He makes it clear that God's power and resources are available to those who believe in Him.' Such people overcome their problems through faith in Jesus Christ and by following Him whatever the cost. The indispensable key as far as he is concerned is that people concentrate on the answer and the victory rather than on the problem and the possibility of defeat. He shows that Christians will only live in victory as they live by the principle of faith taught so consistently by Jesus in His earthly ministry:

Faith in Jesus trusts Him instead of self.
Faith in Jesus believes Him to change the circumstances instead of submitting to problems.
Faith in Jesus believes what He says, instead of doubting His Word.
Faith in Jesus acts on the Word instead of being disobedient.[13]

He also contends that this is not an empty or pious hope because 'faith is the only realistic way of living'. In line with this, he points out that to live by faith is to live in the victory Jesus has *already* won on the Cross:

During his pastoral ministry Jesus overcame sin, sickness and even death. What He did then has been made available to those of any generation who put their faith in Him. The Cross has eternal value for every believer.

Death is God's just and holy judgement on sin. Because He never sinned, Jesus did not deserve to die. He fulfilled completely His Father's will, being obedient to Him in every way, regardless of the cost.

He offered His life as a sacrifice on behalf of sinners. All who grieve the Lord by their sins can know His forgiveness and complete deliverance from guilt. Jesus also took upon Himself all the suffering, affliction and rejection we can experience. He was even oppressed and 'crushed' for us, experiencing complete dereliction on the Cross: 'My God, my God, why have you forsaken me?'[14]

This is possible only in Jesus's name, in submission to the guidance of the Holy Spirit, and through the Word of God. The central idea of victory is then illustrated by reference to many different areas of a Christian's life, including the mind, will, emotions, relationships, spiritual warfare, giving, healing and death.

Personal Victory is comprehensive in range and majors on faith and the dynamic power of the Holy Spirit in overcoming difficulties. One reviewer likened it to a 'school textbook – full of facts, scriptures and a few reasons, but very low on good, nitty-gritty argument'. It is undeniably the case that Colin does not go in for detailed exposition, because he wants to build levels of faith in people by exposing them to vast areas of the Scriptures, thereby challenging them to put their faith into action in their lives: faith without works is dead, as James teaches in his epistle. Put differently, Colin believes that what people need is not human wisdom but divine wisdom, which is to be found in God's Word. He writes: 'The temptation to believe the natural reason rather than the supernatural reason of God will always be with you. Reason limits the Lord in your life; faith releases His activity in your experience.' He is equally decisive on the clash between believing God and trusting to human wisdom a little later in the same chapter:

> God is not opposed to reason; He is beyond reason. His thoughts and ways are much higher than your thoughts and ways. **Do not limit the Lord by your reason**.

> If God says one thing and you say another, someone has to be wrong! Whenever you contradict the Lord you can be sure He is right. He will not change His Word to accommodate your reason or feelings. **It is your ideas and attitudes which will need to change and be brought into line with His truth**.[15]

This viewpoint has been described as rigid, simplistic, non-intellectual, even naive, but Colin's line is consistent: Christians aren't – or shouldn't be – interested in *his* teaching and opinions but in God's Word, which is life-giving and vibrant precisely because the men who wrote it were moved by the Holy Spirit (2 Peter 1:21).

Many people found *Personal Victory* a refreshing book because it is not peppered with quotations from other writers, it is not dominated by personal reminiscences and memories, and because it is encouraging while at the same time being realistic.

My Dear Child (1990) and My Dear Son (1992)

My Dear Child and *My Dear Son* have a number of common characteristics. They symbolise probably the most significant aspect of Colin's Christian life: 'Listening to God's Heart', as the sub-title of *My Dear Child* puts it. Both books are written 'from the heavenly Father's heart to the hearts of his children'. Clearly this is not scripture, and it is not intended to stand alongside the Word of God in significance. So what is it? Colin explains in *My Dear Child*: 'Prophecy is one of the gifts of the Holy Spirit: God speaking into the lives of his people. So this book is a form of prophecy.'

In both books, God is speaking to believers in the Lord

Jesus Christ, reflecting a personal relationship between him (the believer) and the Father. Colin's intention in each book is the same: to help individual believers forge an intimate relationship with their heavenly Father. Colin appears as God's mouthpiece as He reveals the nature of His life to his children ('my dear child, my dear son'). So God assures believers that He is faithful, can always, in every circumstance be relied upon:

I don't have to explain my actions or justify myself before men. I am righteous, so I always act righteously. I am love, therefore I always act in love. **I am faithful and I always act faithfully**.

My dear child, you must understand that I never deny myself. I will never act contrary to my nature. I reveal myself in what I do.

I have always been faithful to you, even when you have been faithless. I have been utterly reliable and dependable. I have been with you always, loving you through every crisis, watching over you with tender care, even when you have been determined to pursue your own course and not mine. I have seen your impatience when I have not answered prayer in the way you wanted; and then later I have seen your relief that I didn't answer you in that way.

People judge me by the failure of my children. But I am never responsible for their sin. I am responsible for their pardon, forgiveness and restoration.

If I was as fickle as some people imagine, this would be a crazy world. There would be no order, only chaos. But I haven't only created by my word: I sustain creation by my word. If I was to be unfaithful to what I have said, the whole universe would go into confusion and chaos.

The reason why there is so much disorder in the world today is because many listen to the lies and deceit of the enemy, placing themselves under his control. He deceives: I am faithful. So I can truly say that heaven and earth will pass away, but my words will not pass away. I watch over them to ensure they are fulfilled.[16]

175

In *My Dear Son* God gives believers a revelation of His love for them, pre-eminently demonstrated by His gift of Jesus:

> Because I love you I sent Jesus to die for **you**. Because I love you I will raise you to my eternal glory. Because I love you I want you for ever.
>
> Please don't doubt my love, beloved. You are forgiven and accepted. There is no need to fear the demands I make on you. You are not a failure; you are my child.
>
> All Jesus' disciples made mistakes; yet all were restored, except the one who had to be lost. You are not a Judas! Unlike him you have received my Spirit, the guarantee that you are mine and have an eternal inheritance.
>
> **I want the very best for you**. Second best is not good enough for you because you are mine! I have a plan for your life just as I had a plan for Jesus. I don't hide from you that at times it will prove costly. It will require the dedication of your whole life. You are to love me wholeheartedly, holding nothing back. What does the cost matter when compared with the benefits?[17]

My Dear Child and *My Dear Son* are unusual books, with God speaking in the first person, a high risk strategy, that is open to misunderstanding. They cover a comprehensive range of subjects. They have both sold in vast numbers. More importantly, they help believers to understand many vital truths in the Bible and are a source of comfort and challenge to the individual believer.

Reasons for success

Many observers are baffled by the commercial success of Colin Urquhart's books. To take but one example, *My Dear Child* was placed second in the 'Top Ten Books of the Year' of 1991 published in the *Church of England Newspaper*, with only *View From A Bouncy Castle* (Adrian Plass) ahead of it. It was placed fourth in the *European Christian Bookstore Journal*, behind *Unexpected Healing* (Jennifer Rees Larcombe), *The New Archibishop Speaks* (George Carey) and *View From A Bouncy Castle* (Plass), though it is worth remembering that best-seller lists are not necessarily a reliable indicator. *My Dear Child* was reprinted five times within the first six months. Colin's success is frustrating for those more naturally talented, who can write more fluently, or who are more theologically educated. There is nothing remotely sophisticated about his books, indeed a number of them are artless in approach and method. Yet, the fact remains that they work, they influence people, help them and affect their behaviour. What, then, explains Colin's success as an author?

Simplicity

Being simple must not be confused with being simplistic (though undeniably Colin's books sometimes are simplistic). What is meant by simplicity is directness of intention, an uncluttered approach devoid of any temptation to be clever or to impress readers. This appeals to the 'ordinary' reader, who wants to be informed and helped so that he can live more purposefully as a Christian in today's world. Allied to this is the fact that Colin comes across as an ordinary man, but one whom God has used. The implication of this is that what's possible for him is also possible for any other man or woman who bothers to listen to God and to act upon what He says.

Humility

Colin's essential humility shines through his writing. There's no parading of the knowledge he's gleaned from various sources; he simply writes what God gives him. One reviewer put it like

177

this: 'Whatever one might think of the quality of his prose, he is a man who has something to say, because he has not neglected to spend time listening to God despite a very active Christian life. Many charismatics and evangelical high-flyers give the impression of being the Christian equivalent of the business tycoon – plenty of hype, wads of notes and glossy presentation. The text of the Bible is preached, but the God of the Bible has to play second fiddle to the high-profile leader. Colin Urquhart, like Billy Graham, has stayed humble before God.'

Subject-matter

Colin is concerned to give people practical material that helps them in their walk before God. The best way to achieve this is to bring his readers into as much contact as possible with the Word of God, the daily feeding which creates faith and stability in men and women so that they become more effective in proclaiming the kingdom of God and expanding it. His books, as shown already, are overwhelmingly biblical in subject-matter and are permeated by Colin's confidence in God. He expresses this confidence in *Holy Fire*:

> There is no situation too powerful, no problem too great, no need too desperate, no bondage too heavy to be dealt with by hearing God speak His Word to your heart. This is how so much of the negative is removed from our lives. When we respond positively to what He says, the Word becomes as fire that purges, cleanses, delivers and heals.[18]

Faith

Because he is a man of faith, Colin brings every activity under God's guidance and direction, with prayer, and with the confidence that God will bless him as He is a God who delights to give good things to His children. He approaches his writing in this way, too.

Relevance

Colin addresses issues that concern people: prayerfulness (or the lack of it), holiness (or a proneness to sin), victory in Christ (or defeat and disillusionment), faith (or its opposite, presumption), and so on. Selwyn Hughes once told me that his daily Bible reading notes, *Every Day With Jesus*, meet people's needs because they 'scratch where people itch'; much the same could be said about Colin's books. An additional factor is that in some of his books he links these facets of Christian living to his own life and experience, and the autobiographical element undoubtedly appeals to men and women fighting the fight of faith.

Anointing

From a literary point of view, there are more gifted writers, but whereas most books are the result of wide-ranging research, voluminous reading and natural talents, Colin's books flow from his close walk with Christ. This factor in my opinion, binds all the previous reasons together. An anointing rests on his books as it does on the spoken word. Colin's writing promotes faith in a confused, troubled and uncertain world. As Edward England said, 'My own faith has grown as a result of every encounter with him. Colin's experience of praying in faith for provision for his college and his community, with a sure confidence that his God-given expectation would be met, has inspired me.' It is precisely because Colin Urquhart is a 'man of the Spirit' that his books sell and affect people's lives in marked ways, whereas those of patently more able men and women struggle to find a market. It is because Colin's books are designed to lead people to faith, to glorify God and be occupied with Him, that an anointing rests upon them. It's as simple as that.

12

THE MAN

The greater part of Colin Urquhart's life is lived before the gaze of other people. To live in community, as he does now and has done for many years, involves a very considerable element of being permanently 'on show', with other people constantly looking to him for help, direction and guidance. Inevitably he is the centre and focus of attention at big meetings, celebrations and conventions. On such occasions, there is more than just the platform separating him from people eager to hear what he has to say; a sense of personal anointing both divides him from the congregation, and equips Colin to declare God's Word and to comfort the people. This anointing is the product of attuning his mind, heart and spirit to the inner promptings of 'the still small voice' of the Holy Spirit. On the public platform Colin is a dominating, confident and authoritative figure, doing what he feels God has called him to do: to preach the 'unsearchable riches of Christ', so that men and women are uplifted, edified, built up and generally equipped to live the life of faith in a robust, uncompromising way.

In this chapter, however, the spotlight is not on the public figure but on a much more personal question: what sort of man is Colin Urquhart?

The boy

Colin's upbringing and childhood was a perfectly normal one living, as he did, in an ordinary family beset with the problems, difficulties and tensions that affect all families. His parents were both strong people, possessed of definite convictions, particularly of the importance of honesty and integrity. They had very specific views regarding the behaviour of their children.

Colin's mother had had a Victorian-type upbringing and was intent on doing the 'proper thing' as a person, as a mother, and as a member of her community. She would, for example, insist on serving a three course meal at night, with a starched white cloth on the table, even when the food itself was limited, barely reaching to three courses. This feature of his mother's precision and correct decorum was not always appreciated by Colin, and his brother was closer to her in emotional terms.

Mr Urquhart was equally determined, though in different ways. He decided to educate all of his three children privately, a decision that involved not only a considerable outlay of money over many, many years but also a very great deal of sacrifice on the part of himself and his wife. It meant, for one thing, living in a very small flat. The bedroom shared by Colin and his brother measured eight feet by eight feet, which meant that the boys had no option but to sleep in bunk-beds. In fact, such was the enormity of the Urquhart parents' sacrifice that they continued to live in an unpretentious flat for over forty years, only buying a house in retirement. The Urquharts were devoted parents who always tried to do their best for their children, something all three recognise today.

Colin was a normal boy, subject to the changes and fluctuations of behaviour and mood like anyone else. The Urquharts were not a noticeably religious family, but Barry (Colin's brother) recalls a significant event when Colin was seven: 'One evening Mother was out on the balcony of the flat listening to the church bells nearby ringing in preparation for Evensong.

Quite suddenly, and without any preamble or fuss, Colin said that he was going to church and, in spite of the family's surprise, even incredulity, did so.'

Barry also recalls another important incident at this formative stage in his brother's life: 'One night we were in our bedroom when I turned to talk to Colin who stopped me and said firmly: '"Be quiet, I'm praying".'

As Colin grew into a teenager, he became very quiet as a person, an introvert or, in psychological terms, remote. He was dubbed the 'Dark Horse' by the other members of the family because they were never sure what he was thinking. On one issue, however, his views were made patently clear to his family. He told them that although he was currently working in an architect's office, he 'had to work for God'. His father, though ashen-faced, said: 'If that's how you feel, you must do it.' So he took the necessary steps to make this decision become a reality.

The student

Colin was not a specially gifted or exceptional student, certainly not a high-flier academically, or the type destined to obtain a 'First'. Unusually, too, for an undergraduate, he spent a lot of time in prayer, listening to God's voice. He lived at home, which meant that his college life was not vastly different from his life previously while at school and work. Later, of course, he lived away from home while pursuing a pastoral year at Warminster. He followed his studies in a quiet way, and played as much cricket as he possibly could in the summer term. As a student Colin seems to have avoided the worst excesses of behaviour traditionally associated with undergraduate life. His career as a student was part of what he felt, quite definitely, was God's plan for his life.

The husband

In the early years of their marriage, particularly at St Hugh's, Colin was perhaps not especially sensitive to Caroline and the many demands upon her time and energies. Today he is much more caring in this respect, and is always prepared to help with domestic chores. Recently I accompanied him on a ministry trip to a town on the south coast, and it was Colin who cut the sandwiches for lunch. He is obviously a concerned and devoted husband, but not in any exaggerated or overtly demonstrative manner. He highly values Caroline's contribution to the overall harmony of the family home, listens seriously to her views, and deeply appreciates her consistently whole-hearted support of his ministry and work at Roffey. There is a calmness and gentle trust about their relationship that is impressive.

The father

Claire, Clive and Andrea value their relationship with both parents as being normal and unexceptional. Claire feels that she can talk to her father 'about anything', but that she has to pick her time carefully to discuss the issue that may be concerning her. She feels too that he is a 'very protective father', generous, and always ready to meet a need. Clive is grateful that, unlike most teenagers, he did not go through the stage of hating or despising his father. He is grateful, too, that his father taught him discipline and the need for clear boundaries in matters of behaviour and morals, as well as the spiritual principle that God is each person's provider and source of supply, and that God is our friend and interested in each of us individually and personally. Clive also feels that he can always be himself with his father, not needing to pretend or act.

Of all three children Andrea has probably needed Colin most, but she is also the one who found living in community the most difficult to come to terms with. She is also the one most prepared to challenge Colin's assertions and views on a whole range of subjects. All three children recognise that their father isn't interested in 'small talk' or gossip, and seldom talks intimately with them – not that these two are to be considered as one and the same. He has consistently taught them the lessons of faith, to be careful about their attitudes to other people, especially when in disagreement, and not to think emotionally.

Claire, Clive and Andrea see their father as a person of integrity, trustworthy, humble, generous, perhaps above all as a man of deep principles who is not prepared to compromise on fundamental matters of faith, Christian practice and behaviour. Nor is he, in their perception, materialistically-minded. Equally clearly, they accept that he is not a natural talker or conversationalist, which can occasionally lead to tensions within the family unit as a whole.

Their relationship with their father is founded on a deep respect, on an acceptance of the fact that he is an extremely busy man with lots on his mind, and on a recognition that God comes – and always will come – first in Colin's life. They know, too, that God is his resource in every situation, be it family, work, preaching, writing or pleasure. They see Colin and Caroline as examples and rôle models for their own lives, both in terms of their marriage and in the rearing of children. By this they mean that the spiritual principles which govern the lives of Colin and Caroline are important and valuable to them as they forge their own relationships with God and, in Claire and Clive's case, bring up their children. They see in their parents an integrity which they aspire to.

The private individual

Colin is not the easiest person to know. In fact, he is shy and retiring, hardly ever talks about himself, or offers his opinions on matters social, political, economic. His personality is quiet and unthreatening, but he can be humorous and sensitive, too. What he finds difficult is to make friends, as distinct from working amicably and constructively with his team. This is so because Colin always seems to preserve a 'sense of distance' between himself and even his closest colleagues and fellow-workers.

Some, like Charles Sibthorpe, would say that he is an enigmatic figure. He says:

> We would go away together on ministry trips, travel, pray and have a good and productive time together, with a time of close fellowship. We would drive together and talk easily about cricket and our families. However, when we'd arrive back at The Hyde, Colin would walk past me in the corridors without greeting me or, in fact, saying anything at all!

Charles found this surprising, as he did Colin's lack of warmth in normal human relations. It may well be the reason why Colin has few close friends, and undeniably he does not find it easy to communicate readily with other people. Others see him as a 'loner' who hides – and quite deliberately so – his innermost feelings from others.

Colin himself responds to this viewpoint in two ways. In the first place, he accepts that he is a loner in the sense that his life revolves around hearing God for himself first, so that he can speak with conviction and authority to others. He sees this as singleness of purpose, not a deliberate attempt to cultivate independence. Living with a sense of God's call, he knows he must be uncompromising in hearing from God, so that he can speak without favour or bias. Above all, perhaps, Colin wants to be a person whom God can trust and use. This necessitates a process of drawing aside, on a daily basis, which causes some people to perceive Colin as being remote and distant. In the second place, Colin points to the fact that the basis of his life and ministry has been that of community life, a cardinal principle of which is a sharing of one's life with other men and women. What I think he fails to understand is that others do not have his single-mindedness and intensity of purpose, so that they must be forgiven for not quite realising and appreciating this daily aspect of his ministry. Thus, they misinterpret his lack of companionability as a device on his part to avoid close contact, while he doesn't fully appreciate the effect he has on others by his quietness and, at times, silence, which can be threatening.

An essentially private person, therefore, it is not surprising that he is passionately fond of cricket and painting, both solitary pursuits in their own way.

The man of God

No assessment of Colin Urquhart would be complete without reference to his qualities and attributes as a man of God, which is essentially how this biography reveals him. However critically certain aspects of his ministry and preaching may be viewed (and inevitably he has his detractors), few fair-minded observers would deny his spiritual stature. Many comment upon his close walk with God. Michael Barling, a colleague of many years, who has observed Colin in various situations at home and abroad, says: 'He really does have an intimate walk with God. Many speakers claim that they "only need the Lord", but when Colin says it, he means it.' Everything is subordinated to his relationship with God and, to quote Barling again, 'If all else were removed from Colin, he would survive.' This impressive personal walk with God has an accompanying dynamic and anointing which gives his life an edge and sharpness that has not diminished with the passing years. It is Colin's intention to please God by thought, word and deed. As a man of God, Colin spends many hours praying, not as a duty or from compulsion, but because it is an integral part of his life. He believes absolutely the promise of Scripture that 'they who pray shall

mount up as on eagle's wings', and that a victorious prayer life
is the result of faith and obedience. Time and again, in his
sermons and books, he illustrates this principle by reference to
Mark 11:24: 'Therefore I tell you, whatever you ask in prayer,
believe that you have received it *and it will be yours*' (Colin's
emphasis. He counters the objection that praying in this spirit
is merely an attempt to dictate to God by saying: 'It is trusting
Him to keep His word, knowing in your heart that He will.' He
frequently emphasises the need to pray 'in the name of Jesus'
which, according to Colin, 'means that you bring Him into the
prayer. He prays along with you. He approaches the problem
with you. You face it together, in His power, with His faith,
that mustard-seed faith that moves mountains.'[1]

The hours Colin spends in prayer indicates his heart's desire
to be holy. He has a luminous spiritual integrity and honesty, to
which those who have lived with him would testify. Everything
in his life grows out of his personal relationship with God which,
ultimately, is a relationship based on the Cross of the Lord Jesus
Christ. It is a relationship controlled by obedience to the Word
of God, with God as Father, motivated by love, and expressing
itself in faith.

Colin exudes an air of tough self-reliance, a sense of wholeness, if you like. Secure in his relationship with God, he
genuinely does believe that to be 'with God' in an ultimate
sense is incomparably better than his present earthly existence.
He does not see death as an enemy but as a gateway to future
glory. At his own Mother's funeral, for example, he spoke
about rejoicing, and said that his Mother was now where he
most wanted to be and that he was envious of her. For most
Christians to say this would be an exaggeration: in Colin's case
it is simply true.

Colin's relationship with God grows out of listening to Him.
People often ask him how he knows when God speaks to him.
They wonder if he hears an audible voice, or if he finds it
difficult to distinguish between his own feelings, God's voice,

or the voice of Satan. He responds to such questioning by saying that he invariably has a quiet but very positive witness when God is speaking directly to him. His confidence is irrefutable:

> Somehow I know it is the Lord. He may be speaking through the Bible, in a time of prayer, in a sermon, or simply through someone in conversation. At the same time, I experience a grave disquiet if what I am hearing is not from God. I am not at peace if my thoughts, even, are not right. If I say something that is wrong I experience immediate correction from the Holy Spirit and have to amend what was said.[2]

This sounds very subjective, but then, as he says, hearing God must, of necessity, be a subjective experience. In this sense, Colin isn't talking merely of feelings which can, of course, be misleading 'as emotions change so rapidly in response to what is happening around us'. He is absolutely insistent that hearing God is not a feeling rather 'an inner knowing that the Lord has spoken'. Then, having heard subjectively, what is heard has to be tested objectively, which can only be done through the Word of God.

The process of attentive listening is vital to the continued effectiveness of his ministry. He gives an interesting illustration of this in *Faith For The Future*. By the summer of 1977, after he had been travelling regularly for eighteen months, he became aware of a persistent spiritual problem:

> While in Luton, there had been a constant progression in my spiritual life. I had to seek the Lord continually for his direction so that I could lead others in the ways of His Spirit. God was always facing us with new things, new challenges, taking us to new and deeper places with Himself.

> I now realised how much I had missed being part of a body moving on with God. Although I had learned a great deal in the past eighteen months of travelling and had seen Him at work in wonderful ways, yet there was something missing. I was spiritually jaded.[3]

189

He wondered what was lacking. The answer he got was an incisive one:

> The Lord showed me that I had faithfully sought Him for the ministry, but I had stopped seeking Him for Himself. I was no longer breaking through to new places with Him. He wanted to reveal Himself to me in new ways and deepen my understanding of Himself. There were many things that He could then teach me that would make my ministry to others far more fruitful.[4]

He realised that this fresh insight had to be accompanied by action:

> I went carefully through each area of my life, asking the Holy Spirit to show me where repentance was needed. I had disobeyed the Lord in taking on too much ministry. Because of tiredness I had grown lax in spiritual discipline in some ways. I no longer arose for prayer as early as I used to. I had prayed about the ministry but had not interceded in other ways as I could have done. And so on. I wrote all these things down, and other things too: wrong attitudes towards others, neglect of giving to my family because I was so busy. All had to be brought to the cross.

> I knelt and began to pour out all these things to the Lord. As I prayed there was a tremendous sense of the Lord's presence. His peace descended on me; I was completely forgiven. His joy filled my heart and I was bursting to sing God's praises in a way I had not experienced in a long time. I was filled with such gratitude towards Him for His faithfulness; once more He had demonstrated His life and mercy. He had shown again that true repentance always leads to a fresh release of the Holy Spirit's activity in our lives.[5]

To be able as a man of God to minister strength and confidence to others, Colin has to be confident – absolutely – of his own place and position in God; also to deal with anything that would destroy or impair this confidence. He says in *Listen and Live*:

If we are seeking to please the Lord, living by faith in Him, our hearts will not condemn us. We shall not always get everything right, but when we sin or fail we turn to the Lord in His mercy and graciousness and receive forgiveness – not allowing ourselves to feel condemned by the enemy, by others, or by our own sense of failure. We have confidence because we are sure of who God, is, the Faithful One who is perfect love, for whom nothing is impossible; the One in whom we live, and move and have our being. It is so important to ensure you are right with God and others, that nothing may destroy your confidence in Him.[6]

A complementary truth he often expounds is that Christians have all the resources necessary for sharing God's love and power with other people, notably a 'sound mind':

Self-discipline is part of the fruit of the Holy Spirit (Gal. 5:23), one of the qualities He produces in the believer. The Amplified Bible translates this as having a 'well balanced mind and discipline and self-control'. You are able to be in control of your thinking and do not have to receive the fearful, negative, accusing, condemning thoughts that the enemy wants to plant in your mind. If you think correctly, you will act in accordance with God's will. *You have a spirit of self-discipline*, a sound mind.

Your mind is not to be the plaything of the enemy. This is his first line of attack. Yes, he knows that if he can encourage you to think incorrectly then you will also speak and act incorrectly. By contrast, the Holy Spirit informs your mind of God's thoughts, reminding you of His Words. In every situation He wants you to be attentive to His voice. It is so important, therefore, to receive His Words and to store them within your heart.[7]

As a man of God, Colin's grasp of biblical truth is extensive. His knowledge is the product of the Holy Spirit's operation in his life, and his study of Scripture. There is no other explanation, for he wasn't steeped in evangelical theology, while his theological training at King's College was academic, sceptical, rational, and not intended to create faith in the reliability and dependability of the Word of God. In theological terms, he was unread, an illiterate, who at the beginning of his ministry felt threatened by the prospect of having to preach several times each Sunday, so limited was his knowledge of the Bible. The Holy Spirit had to be Colin's teacher and guide in matters of truth and biblical knowledge.

It was at St Hugh's, Luton, particularly in the first Bible study group, that the result of the Holy Spirit's teaching in Colin's life began to be felt on a corporate level. He recalls: 'The Word of God was coming to life for every member of that group, all of whom had been filled with the Spirit. God was revealing His truth to us.' This transformation in attitude and perception applied as powerfully to the Old Testament as it did to the New Testament. Discovering what God was saying in the Bible became, for Colin, and by extension for those he led, 'an adventure in itself': As the Bible came alive for St Hugh's, so 'signs and wonders' (in the form of healings, speaking in tongues, openness to God's Spirit, and risk-taking) were operative long before the advent in England of the 'Third Wave' of the charismatic movement and the influence of the American evangelist John Wimber.

Bob Roxburgh, in his book *Renewal Down to Earth*,[8] observes that an absolutely essential ingredient in renewal is not just the phenomenon of healings and miracles, but the overall spiritual dimension that nurtures it; and that the Bible is the key to the whole process. Colin had to push back the frontiers himself before the congregation at St Hugh's could follow him in a spirit of freshness and expectancy. He would not have achieved this without listening avidly, daily and determinedly to what God was saying to him. This is all-important for understanding the life and motivation of Colin Urquhart: he is first and foremost a man of faith.

13

INTO THE NINETIES

The nineteen eighties were years of unceasing activity for Colin. The decade began with the localised revival at The Hyde which gave him a glimpse into the essence of revival, and it continued with the growth of the Bethany Fellowship and the arrival of men such as Bob Gordon. By the end of the eighties Bob Gordon, Charles Sibthorpe and David Brown had all moved away from West Sussex, leaving Colin and Michael Barling as the only two remaining elders. The latter part of the decade had not been easy for Colin, or for those who supported his ministry, and he could have been forgiven for thinking that the best years were behind him.

To take this view would, however, be to ignore a fundamental part of his make-up as a Christian: he always looks to the future. In fact, towards the end of 1990 and the beginning of 1991 he felt a new and vibrant stirring within himself: the distinct feeling that the time had come to move into the work for which the years at Cheshunt and Letchworth initially, then the years at St Hugh's and The Hyde, were a preparation: widespread revival. This feeling also confirmed for Colin that the 'real thing' in his life was about to be revealed. It is in this context that reference must be made to three special developments which are of significance both for Colin's own ministry and for that of the work he directs.

Spirit of Faith Ministries

Launched in August 1990, 'Spirit of Faith Ministries' has at its core an emphasis on God's dynamic of faith, which Colin defines as a 'steady confidence in God which is not affected by external circumstances. Such a faith changes the circumstances.' He believes that Spirit of Faith Ministries was 'born out of an initiative taken by the Lord. Those involved believe very firmly that they are responding to a call from God.'

Spirit of Faith Ministries (under the umbrella of Kingdom Faith Ministries) has several definite purposes. It aims, first, to link the concepts of 'faith' and 'revival'. Colin believes that God intends there to be a spiritual awakening in this country and that He is preparing for such an event. Before that can happen, however, he knows that there must be a genuine revival within the church itself, and in this process faith is a crucial element. Colin does not see the purpose of SPF as to recall the early days of the charismatic movement, nor even to be identified with that movement as such, but as a ministry to leaders in the nation. He explains the reasons behind his thinking like this:

> During the past twenty years or so, the church in this country has been greatly blessed through the charismatic move of God which has developed and deepened. However, it must also be acknowledged that much of the early fire has been lost. Where is the simplicity of faith which accompanied the early move of God? It seemed then that healings and miracles abounded far more than one hears about today. There was an enthusiasm and a joy through people meeting with Jesus and having their lives transformed. This enthusiasm has been maintained in some places but lost in others . . .

> The joyful enthusiasm and devotion to Jesus needs not only to be restored but increased. This will need to be expressed in true evangelistic zeal. This in turn will be expressed in prayer for the lost, coupled with a genuine repentance on behalf of the people of this land.

Repentance is not enough. The call of Jesus Christ is to repent and believe. In recent years there has been a move of repentance on behalf of the nation. Now we need to see the move of faith.[1]

A second aim of Spirit of Faith Ministries is to foster deeper dimensions of faith. 'Our faith', says Colin, 'must be in what He says.' This will lead not only to dependence on God's Word but a more realistic and Christ-like life-style, with an accompanying effectiveness in prayer and more powerful ministry. The logic of Colin's position is clear:

God has brought us to fullness of life in Christ and has given us everything we need for life and godliness. We lack no good thing and nothing is able to separate us from His love. We have His Word which is more enduring than heaven and earth, and we have His Spirit living in us. All the resources of the kingdom of God are made available to us. So why do we not manifest more of the life, power and victory of Jesus?

The conclusion is obvious. There needs to be vibrant faith in the Word of God and in what He has done. We need the faith of God which translates theory into positive expression in our lives.

For many years I was perplexed, as I travelled the world and rubbed shoulders with some of the leading men of God who are household names, as to why some of them manifested a dimension of faith that was foreign to others. This does not mean, of course, that they lacked faith. They would not have anointed international ministries unless their faith in Jesus Christ was real and active. It is simply that some trusted God in a way that others did not . . .

We need the faith with which to do it and the willingness for our lives to be laid on the line. By faithful obedience to the leading of God's Spirit we will do the things He tells us to do. We will not back away with fear. With boldness and confidence born of faith in Jesus Christ we will see the purposes of God fulfilled in our nation.[2]

A third aim of Spirit of Faith Ministries is to prepare for

revival. 'Revival' is defined as 'a divine attack upon society' and as 'the restoration of Truth again'. This is the vision that undergirds all that takes place at Roffey Place, where students and team members are enouraged to prepare for revival-type ministries, and also to be men and women who will be absolutely uncompromising in their discipleship to bring this about. Each day at Roffey (from 7.00 a.m. to 10.00 p.m.) there is a continuous chain of prayer for the nation. This 'hidden work' is seen as vital if the task of revival – to change the climate in society, to oppose the Devil totally, to crush his initiative, and to invade the nations with the power of God publicly – is to be achieved. It is the work to which Colin has committed himself without reserve or compromise. It is the desire of his heart: the fire of God burning in his heart with total persuasion and conviction.

Revival at Roffey Place

Early in 1992 there were 'times of refreshing' at Roffey Place. This was the third time that Colin had experienced localised revival in his ministry, following St Hugh's and The Hyde. The three experiences were, however, quite different. At Luton, the church responded to his leading as he came into one revelation of God after another, almost in a non-stop way. He knew little historically about revival, he had not experienced it himself before. At that time, revival for Colin meant 'having a fresh revelation of Jesus Christ and responding to it'.

At The Hyde, God brought about the revival in the community by meeting with the people in His holiness and power. Colin has likened it to 'Pentecost', and part of its fruit was seen in the locality (the setting up of prayer groups for example), and in the courses for leaders at The Hyde. In 1981 Colin was something of a lone voice in charismatic circles in his insistence on the need for revival. There were those, too, in the historic denominations who felt that it had to be a denominational revival and they objected to Colin sometimes appearing to be a Free Church Pastor in the cloak of an Anglican clergyman. Colin felt that for this reason the revival at The Hyde could not impact the nation in any discernible manner.

At Roffey Place in 1992, there was a further element in the revival there: the community, those associated with it and the students, sought to enter into revival by faith, through seeking God for themselves, together with the very real feeling that now is God's time to affect the nation. Colin feels that he has to be obedient to this heavenly vision. The full breakthrough has not come yet, but there can be no turning back from what God has revealed, which has particular relevance to the third development.

Kingdom Faith Church

The development of the Kingdom Faith Church is likely to be the most controversial area of all, although Colin is not now a minister of the Church of England. His co-pastor, Dan Chesney, has described the thinking behind the founding of this church in April 1992:

> I felt an urgency to pray. I went up to my room and prayer came easily. I found myself repeating the words 'revival centre' and I could see the centre clearly in my mind. It consisted of a large church, a Bible school, a resource centre, ministry teams and leadership training facilities. From this centre other churches, ministries and Bible schools were being born throughout Britain and beyond. It was like a spiritual power station and generating other lighthouses all round the world . . . With this vision still vivid in my mind, Colin Urquhart and I met one week later. As we talked we discovered God had been speaking to both of us in this way.[3]

Several months of prayer followed until November 1991, when

a meeting of the Kingdom Faith fellowship was called to announce that a church would officially begin. A core group of about a hundred people came together, and by February 1992 the number had grown to a hundred and forty people. The vision for the church was made abundantly clear from the start: men and women living in revival, prepared to lay down their lives for one another in love, committed to a life of faith in God's Word, walking in the light and bringing the truth to the world. Those who intended becoming members of the Kingdom Faith Church were expected to assent in writing to this vision. As Dan Chesney says, 'Only through this dynamic of faith, holiness, love and evangelism would the area and the nation be impacted. A longing for revival was to be at the heart of the church. Only as the Holy Spirit moves through a body of believers in revival power can we hope to see the nation turned back to righteousness.'[4]

There then followed three weeks of revival meetings, with three hours spent each day in prayer before the public meetings took place. At the end of this period people were invited to make a public commitment to the Lord, to the vision of revival, and to each other. The church grew rapidly once again, this time to approximately three hundred people, and it continues to grow weekly with people being converted and with others catching the vision. By July 1993 there were over 600 in membership, with at least 800 people worshipping at Roffey Place each Sunday. A spiritual impetus has been created within a twenty-five mile radius of Roffey Place, and the hope is that it will extend further into the life of the nation.

Colin Urquhart and Dan Chesney are confident that they are in the will of God as far as Kingdom Faith Church is concerned. They face the rest of the decade with a confidence born of faith and the influence of the Holy Spirit.

14

LOOKING BACK, LOOKING FORWARD

Colin Urquhart is well into his sixth decade of life and into his fourth decade as a minister of the gospel. His career so far has been a notable and highly influential one. He is held in high respect by people across the denominational spectrum. His preaching services and celebrations still attract large numbers of people, while the Faith Camps (currently held in Peterborough each summer) continue to draw huge crowds of people, with up to seven thousand men and women coming from all over the world. At these camps people are converted, backsliders are restored, healings occur, and people's faith levels are increased and deepened. The community and church he leads at Roffey Place seem to be thriving, while his writing is in as much demand as ever. To explain the patent success of his life and ministry we shall need to look back and forward.

Looking back

As he looks back on his life, Colin never ceases to marvel at the way God has led him so far. He began his spiritual life as an Anglo-Catholic with very little knowledge of the Bible, but as he has submitted himself to the discipline of God's Word he has become a faith warrior who looks to God for blessing, direction and the supply of all his needs: material, financial, personal. His life exemplifies the dictum that when a person truly and genuinely seeks God first, all the other things will be added as well. Ultimately Colin's life and ministry prove that God is a faithful, loving heavenly Father who honours His word, and who delights in blessing His children.

In this context, Colin frequently returns to three metaphors in his preaching and writing. There is, in the first instance, the idea of a God who is faithful. The Father God assures his dear child:

> You must understand that I never deny myself. I will never act contrary to my nature. I reveal myself in what I do.
>
> I have always been faithful to you, even when you have been faithless. I have been utterly reliable and dependable. I have been with you always, loving you through every crisis, watching over you with tender care, even when you have been determined to pursue your own course and not mine.[1]

In the second place, this faithful God is someone who fills His people with His own power:

> My Holy Spirit is supernatural and brings both love and power into your life; he enables you to live the life of my Kingdom. Jesus said, 'You will receive power when the Holy Spirit comes on you.' So, my child, I want you to realise that you are filled with power. Yes, you really are. You rarely feel full of power, do you? Nevertheless, all the resources of my supernatural power are available to you, and are at work within you.[2]

Then, in the third place is the fact that this faithful and powerful God also asks of each individual Christian this searching question:

> How much of you belongs to me? Everything. *All of you*. You are mine for ever.
>
> I have paid the price for you, haven't I? I didn't purchase

part of you with my Son's blood. I purchased the whole of you because I wanted every part of you. So you really are my property, child.

How much of you do I possess in practice? I know every part of you belongs to me, but do you really surrender every part of yourself? Do you still want your own plans and purposes, instead of mine? You know the answers, child. *But just as I am encouraging you to take possession of every part of me, so I am taking possession of every part of you.*[3]

Looking back, it is apparent that Colin's commitment to God has grown and matured over the years. It is this appreciation of God, this desire to please him, this abandonment to God which is the key to an understanding of his life and work. He is dedicated to God, and his whole life is committed to His service. Colin wants his words to reflect the God of Glory – His holiness, love, compassion, generosity, power – and his life to be an instrument in the extension of His kingdom. He lives his life in the sure and certain knowledge that he is himself destined for glory. His attitude may be summed up in this way: 'God's Word reveals who He is, what He has done for us in Jesus and what He wants of us. We have to choose to obey or disobey; to believe or contradict what he says.'[4] Faith is, after all, a matter of choice, and looking back it is the principle by which Colin has ruled his life in its many and varied aspects.

Looking forward

Much as he is conscious of God's leading the past, Colin is not bound to the past: he is not its prisoner, hemmed in and restricted either by the past's failures or successes. One of the reasons for this is that the principles of faith which have operated in the past will be those by which he regulates his life in the future, too. Another reason is that he is not content to accept the *status quo*, to settle down to a comfortable life, resting on his laurels. He has great expectations for the future.

The starting-point is his belief that God desires to give every Christian man, woman and child faith for the future. He means by this the belief that in the coming years God is going to move among His people in greater power than hitherto. It involves accepting that God wants to give us all His faith and teach us to see things with His perspective. This will also mean coming to the end of compromise in our lives as God calls us to belong to Him, to be part of His building, the body, as He fulfils His promise to build the church, against which not even the gates of Hades can prevail.

The second reason that Colin can look forward to the future with confidence is that God has proved himself so miraculously to him in the past, that he knows He can do so again, if only he continues to be obedient.

The third reason has to do with the vision of revival that he has had. He outlined his thinking regarding the future in a sermon at Roffey Place in March 1992 entitled 'God *is* coming to the nation', taking as his text the prophecy of Habakkuk, a contemporary of Jeremiah. The prophet was called to speak to a nation drastically in need of revival, spiritually, socially and politically. Israel needed a fresh visitation from God; and the people themselves needed to be inspired to pray for the state of the nation. The parallel with Britain – indeed the rest of the world – is not difficult to work out:

> God is coming to Britain, to save. God wants a church moving in His saving power. He can cause rivers to flow in a spiritual wilderness. The rain of the Lord can fall here and the river will flow hundreds of miles. We can say this because we've heard from God. Having heard from Him, it would be faithless not to declare this. The coming revival will be a time of victory and wholeness in Jesus.

There are many equally sincere Christian leaders who would

hesitate to proclaim their understanding or perceptions in such an unequivocal manner. Amongst this number are some of Colin's own close associates. That is not the issue. What is much more significant is that Colin has heard God for himself, and is prepared to trust, without reserve or qualification, what he has heard. This is the secret to his success as a Christian and as a leader.

Colin's unshakeable conviction means that he lives with a sense of enormous responsibility: he is called by God to experience revival, and to be a catalyst in helping to bring it about. This divine propulsion is exciting, too, and he looks to the future with buoyant enthusiasm and fresh expectancy. As always, his attitude, a thoroughly biblical one, is that the best is yet to be. This recognition works in two ways. It can look back and pinpoint the grace of God in bringing him thus far, accepting his guidance and bountiful supply with gratitude and wonder. It can, at the same time, look forward to the future with even greater expectancy in the light of God's goodness in the past, and with heightened confidence that He will be true to His Word. Colin Urquhart's story is an unfinished one: it will always be thus because he is constantly looking to the future with God.

ABBREVIATIONS

The following abbreviations are used frequently in the Notes:

AYA: Anything You Ask
FFF: Faith for the Future
HF: Holy Fire
ICJ: In Christ Jesus
LL: Listen and Live
MDC: My Dear Child
MDC My Dear Son
MFG: My Father is the Gardener
PV: Personal Victory
RYH: Receive Your Healing
TPK: The Positive Kingdom
WSC: When the Spirit Comes

All these titles are published by Hodder & Stoughton.

NOTES

Introduction

1 *When the Spirit Comes* (1974), *My Father is the Gardener* (1977), *Anything You Ask* (1978), *In Christ Jesus* (1981), *Faith for the Future* (1982), *Holy Fire* (1984), *The Positive Kingdom* (1985), *Receive Your Healing* (1986), *Listen and Live* (1987), *Personal Victory* (1988), *My Dear Child* (1990), *My Dear Son* (1992); all published by Hodder & Stoughton
2 *TPK*, pp.116–17.

Chapter One

1 *WSC*, p.11.
2 *TPK*, p.116.

Chapter Two

1 *RYH*, p.20.
2 Caroline Urquhart, *His God, My God* (Hodder & Stoughton, 1983), p.34.

3 Watchman Nee, *The Normal Christian Life* (Victory Press, 1957), p.76.
4 *Normal Christian Life*, p.77.
5 *WSC*, p.9.
6 *PV*, p.54.

Chapter Three

1 *WSC*, p.16.
2 *WSC*, p.16.
3 *WSC*, p.16.
4 *WSC*, p.18.
5 *WSC*, pp.20–1.
6 *WSC*, pp.27–8.
7 *WSC*, p.31.
8 *WSC*, p.32.
9 *WSC*, p.44.
10 *WSC*, p.95.
11 *WSC*, p.117.
12 *WSC*, p.117.
13 *WSC*, pp.117–21.
14 *WSC*, p.126.
15 *WSC*, p.126.
16 *WSC*, p.41.
17 *WSC*, p.63.
18 *WSC*, pp.103–4.

Chapter Four

1 See pp.10–11.
2 Lord Runcie communicated his views to the author in a series of letters.

3 Teddy Saunders and Hugh Sansom, *David Watson* (Hodder & Stoughton, 1992).
4 From a letter to the author.
5 From a letter to the author.

Chapter Five

1 *His God, My God*, p.18.
2 *His God, My God*, p.36.
3 *His God, My God*, p.26.
4 *His God, My God*, p.53.

Chapter Six

1 *FFF*, p.27.

Chapter Seven

1 *FFF*, pp.90–1.
2 *AYA*, p.1.
3 *FFF*, p.118.
4 *FFF*, p.122.
5 See 2 Corinthians 5:17, for example.

Chapter Eight

1 *FFF*, p.173.
2 *FFF*, p.173.
3 *FFF*, pp.177–80.
4 Charles Sibthorpe, *A Man Under Authority* (Kingsway, 1984), p.60.

5 *A Man Under Authority*, p.61.

Chapter Nine

1 Bob Gordon, *Out of the Melting Pot* (Marshalls, 1984) p.11.
2 *TPK*, p.99.
3 *Out of the Melting Pot*, p.25.
4 *TPK*, p.100.
5 *TPK*, p.101.
6 *TPK*, p.102.
7 *TPK*, p.102.
8 *Out of the Melting Pot*, p.32.
9 *Out of the Melting Pot*, p.72.
10 *TPK*, p.100.
11 *AYA*, p.153.
12 *AYA*, p.153.
13 *AYA*, p.97.
14 *LL*, pp.99–100.

Chapter Ten

1 Edward England (ed.), *My Call To Preach* (Highland Books, 1986), p.149.
2 *My Call*, p.153.
3 *My Call*, p.153.
4 *My Call*, p.154.
5 *My Call*, p.156.
6 *My Call*, p.156.
7 *My Call*, p.157.
8 *My Call*, p.160.
9 Martyn Lloyd-Jones, *Preaching and Preachers* (Hodder & Stoughton, 1971), p.9.

10 *Preaching and Preachers*, p.9.
11 *My Call*, p.161.
12 *My Call*, p.159.
13 *Preaching and Preachers*, p.56.
14 *AYA*, p.103.
15 *ICJ*, p.161.
16 Colin Urquhart, *Our Rich Inheritance* (Kingdom Faith Ministries), p.15.
17 *Our Rich Inheritance*, p.19.
18 *AYA*, p.98.
19 *ICJ*, *p.81*.
20 *AYA*, p.71.
21 *AYA*, pp.72–3.
22 *AYA*, pp.81–2.
23 Colin Urquhart, *Revival is Coming* (Kingdom Faith Ministries), pp.4–5.
24 *Revival is Coming*, pp.6–7.
25 *Revival is Coming*, p.13.
26 *Revival is Coming*, p.14.
27 *HF*, p.51.
28 *HF*, p.89.
29 *HF*, p.196.
30 *Healing and Wholeness* (no.3, July/September 1991).
31 *TPK*, p.117.
32 *TPK*, p.15.
33 *ICJ*, p.29.
34 *ICJ*, p.300.
35 Quoted in John Peters, *Martyn Lloyd-Jones* (Paternoster Press, 1986), p.49.

Chapter Eleven

1 *FFF*, p.49.
2 *MFG*, p.65.

3 *MFG*, pp.136–7.
4 *AYA*, pp.16–17.
5 *AYA*, p.18.
6 *AYA*, p.144.
7 *AYA*, p.182.
8 *ICJ*, pp.80–1.
9 *FFF*, p.202.
10 *TPK*, p.150.
11 *RYH*, p.280.
12 *LL*, pp.69–70.
13 *PV*, p.15.
14 *PV*, p.16.
15 *PV*, p.31.
16 *MDC*, pp.193–4.
17 *MDC*, pp.100–1.
18 *HF*, p.104.

Chapter Twelve

1 *AYA*, p.125.
2 *FFF*, p.11.
3 *FFF*, p.62.
4 *FFF*, p.62.
5 *FFF*, pp.62–3.
6 *LL*, p.217.
7 *LL*, p.128.
8 Bob Roxburgh, *Renewal Down To Earth* (Kingsway Publications, 1987) p.38.

Chapter Thirteen

1 *Spirit of Faith* magazine (now re-named *Kingdom Faith*), January 1991, pp.4–5.

2 *Spirit of Faith*, January 1991, pp.4–5.
3 *Kingdom Faith* magazine, June 1992, p.14.
4 *Kingdom Faith*, June 1992, p.14.

Chapter Fourteen

1 *MDC*, pp.193–4.
2 *MDC*, pp.116–17.
3 *MDC*, pp.171–2.
4 Colin Urquhart, *The Faith Dynamic* (Kingdom Faith Ministries), p.17.

INDEX